Faith and Freedom
A Biographical Sketch of a Great American
John Howard Pew

ALFRED
PANEPINTO
AIA

FAITH AND FREEDOM

The Journal of a Great American
J. Howard Pew

compiled by
Mary Sennholz

Grove City College
Grove City, Pa. 16127
1975

2-24-78

Acknowledgment

When first asked whether I would like to edit the speeches of J. Howard Pew my reply was that I thought it would be fun. But the project has been much more than an enjoyable experience. For almost a year it has meant living with the thoughts and actions of a great man who, as was said of Saul, son of Kish, "From his shoulders and upward he was higher than any of the people."

I owe deep gratitude to Leonard E. Read for his unfailing encouragement at all stages of this work. Thanks are due to Allyn R. Bell, Jr. and W. W. Weston for providing information and helpful suggestions. My appreciation must also be expressed to Paul L. Poirot for his patient editorial labors, and to my husband for his faithful cooperation.

M. S.

Foreword

THE LATE J. HOWARD PEW was once described by a friend of long and close acquaintanceship as "a great American citizen, a man devoted to his country and loving passionately the freedom that he felt was our heritage."

Of all the tributes paid to Mr. Pew, this one, I feel, is the most fitting. And the achievement of *Faith and Freedom* is that it eloquently expresses the beliefs and values and philosophies that shaped this unique American and his contributions to his nation.

I was personally privileged to work for and with Mr. Pew for most of my career in the management of Sun Oil Company. Over a period of almost four decades, I came to know him as a trusted associate, an inspiring leader, a close friend, and a source of professional and personal counsel and advice. Out of that association arose a deep affection for him as an individual, and a sincere appreciation and admiration for his contributions to American business enterprise and to society generally.

In the main thrust of his industrial career, where I knew him best, he was an entrepreneur in the very highest sense of that concept. He was resourceful, purposeful, farseeing, a tough-minded risk-taker. His venturesomeness and vision are directly reflected today in the strength of the Sun organization.

But he was not only an entrepreneur. He was also an accomplished engineer who helped to pioneer technological breakthroughs in petroleum processing that were of immense benefit to all Americans. He early perceived the energy supply pressures that would arise as the world economy grew. And in one response to that realization, he became the driving force in Sun's pioneering breakthrough in commercial production of oil from the vast Athabasca tar sands in Alberta, Canada.

Overshadowing these considerable industrial achievements and his contributions to community and society, however, were the intensely human personal qualities that shaped Mr. Pew's own life and his relationships with others. He was modest, humble, understanding, a man of unyielding integrity and of compassionate concern for his fellows.

He deeply valued and respected the views of others in all things. In management meetings, for example, I often saw him reserve his own views so as not to inhibit the expression of opinions by others.

He was a shrewd, but fair, judge of character, a man given to deliberately testing the fiber of others. As a result, he surrounded himself with competent and trustworthy associates.

He was fiercely loyal, in turn, to his friends and associates, and especially so to the people of Sun Oil Company whose affection and respect he prized.

His modest and simple personal tastes were reflected in the straight chair and plain table that sufficed as office furniture for many years.

He was the personification of integrity in all of his dealings and relationships, a man who sealed agreements with a handshake and whom an acquaintance once characterized as incapable of deceit. A U.S. senator once described him to me as "not only talking like, but looking like, an affidavit."

His humility and reverence were reflected in dedicated service to the congregation of his home church, the Presbyterian church in Ardmore, Pa. He agreed to become an elder of that church only after much searching of his own conscience. And pastor William Faulds, D.D., today recalls Mr. Pew's feeling that, of all the recognition that came to him during his lifetime, there was no greater honor than to serve his Lord as an elder in that congregation.

He was a scholar who read widely and reflected deeply, particularly on the Bible and on the principles of private enterprise.

Out of that scholarship, in his middle and later years, developed a dedication to writing and speaking in support of freedom. His basic thesis was expressed in these words, which I heard him speak often:

> Freedom is indivisible. Once industrial freedom is lost, political freedom, religious freedom and freedom of the press and of speech will also fall.

His most pleasurable personal interest was his long-time association with Grove City College. And in a very real sense, the College, its beautiful campus and the widening educational experiences it offers are a living memorial to Mr. Pew. So it is truly fitting that this account of his life and his philosophies should be written by a member of the Grove City College community.

The readers of *Faith and Freedom* will find much to ponder in the life of J. Howard Pew.

His human warmth, his personal integrity, his religious convictions, his commitment to moral values, his capacity for leadership, his dedication to freedom, his willingness to speak out for what he believed—all of these reflect understanding, acceptance and support for the basic principles upon which this nation was built. In the uncertain present, a re-dedication to those principles of the past could mean much to the strength and stability of our country in the future.

ROBERT G. DUNLOP
Retired Chairman and
Chief Executive Officer
Sun Oil Company

January, 1975

Faith and Freedom
A Biographical Sketch of a Great American
John Howard Pew

Published by Grove City College,
Grove City, Pa. 16127

Typography & Printing by
Sowers Printing Company,
Lebanon, Pa. 17042

One

●

Of Pioneer Stock

NO PLACE IN THE WORLD today is as distant as the American colonies were from England during the 16th and 17th centuries. It took no less than six weeks to cross the Atlantic to America. Travelers faced great dangers of ocean storms on tiny ships rarely weighing more than 200 tons. Cramped in scanty quarters with stale food and water, they suffered untold hardships even before they reached American shores. On many a voyage, of some one hundred passengers which a ship like the *Mayflower* would normally carry, ten to twenty were buried at sea.

On one of such sailing vessels the ancestors of the Pew family, with other English emigrants, arrived in Virginia about 1640. Leaving their home near the border of Wales, they set out for the new world in one of the most turbulent periods of European history.

Charles I of the house of Stuarts was King of England (1625-1649). On the Continent raged the Thirty Years' War, the bloodiest of all general European wars in history. England had been involved since 1620; but after a few unsuccesful expeditions against French and Spanish forces, peace was made with France in 1629 and Spain in 1630. The burden of war had caused King Charles to use every device to raise money for expeditions, make forced loans and arbitrarily imprison many who refused to pay, to billet soldiers for whom the government could not afford to hire quarters, and to impose martial law on the soldiers and civilians around them—all of which had caused great alarm among Englishmen. Moreover, the King's dissolution of Parliament and return to purely conciliar government, royal extravagance, corruption,

1

traffic in titles and wardships, multiplication of grants of
monopoly, had generated bitter discontent and hostility. But
above all, the machinery of government had been used vig-
orously to enforce an unpopular ecclesiastical policy, which
finally led to riots in Scotland, grew into a national revolt,
followed by the Civil War (1642-1648) and King Charles'
trial and execution in 1649. For the next eleven years England, Scotland and Ireland were to become a "commonwealth" under Oliver Cromwell, protector and lord general.

Such were the political conditions which thousands of emigrants chose to leave behind in order to seek a new beginning in another world. Their personal motives and reasons lie
hidden in the distant past. But we do know that by 1640
some 60,000 British subjects, among them the Pews, had em-
igrated to the new world colonies. In New England the Puritan sectaries who had sailed on the *Mayflower* (1620) had
founded the first colony. They were followed by a second Puritan Massachusetts Bay Company (1628), which soon grew
offshoots in Rhode Island, New Hampshire and Connecticut.
Lord Baltimore had established Maryland as a Catholic
refuge in 1634.

In Virginia where the Pews chose to settle, several early attempts at establishing permanent colonies during the reign of
Queen Elizabeth (1558-1603) had failed for various reasons.
One colony on Roanoke Island that seemed to have a prom-
ising future disappeared without a trace. But in 1606 the
Virginia Company, a joint-stock company with a royal charter
to settle the coast of North America, sent three ships with
144 passengers to Virginia and began a settlement at Jamestown, which was to become the first permanent English colony in North America. It remained under control of the Virginia Company until 1624 when the King revoked the company's charter and made it a Royal Colony.

Life at Jamestown was extremely hard in those years. By
1608 disease and privation had reduced the number of orig-

inal settlers to 38. Yet the colony survived and conditions began to improve when the original system of working and sharing produce in common was abandoned and individuals were permitted to own land privately. And in 1619 the morale of the colony improved immeasurably when the Virginia Company sent some ninety young women as wives for the colonists. But thereafter the future of the colony turned cloudy again when in 1622 a series of fierce Indian attacks resulted in the death of some 300 colonists, which together with the plague that followed killed 75 per cent of the population.

The Pew ancestors arrived a few years later. We do not know whether they remained in Jamestown or moved on to the Middle Plantation (now Williamsburg) that had just been founded. Perhaps they settled along the new palisade that crossed the peninsula and provided some protection from Indians as well as a large range for cattle. Perhaps they barely escaped the Indian massacre of 1644 that took the lives of some 500 colonists. For the Pews as well as for many other survivors the sudden attack brought untold horrors of battle with the Indians and painful material destruction which took many years to rebuild.

The first generation of Pews in Virginia faced many more difficulties. Human and cattle plagues ravaged the colony; hurricanes devastated homes, barns, and fields; oppressive royal laws and trade restrictions prevented or retarded economic development; Indian raids required constant alertness and costly preparedness.

With a few exceptions the early pioneers were farmers who tilled the soil with crude implements and some help from animal power. An immigrant would acquire a share in the Virginia Company and receive 50 acres of land as his "headright" simply by coming to Virginia. For each additional member of the family or a servant brought over from England 50 more acres were granted. More headrights could be acquired by purchase from the secretary of the Colony for a few shillings, so that some individuals were able to build up rather large land holdings. But most pioneers owned relatively small farms of no more than 100 acres. They struggled for mere survival against unpredictable nature and hostile Indians. As soon as possible they tried to raise a surplus crop that could be marketed for better farming tools, some gunpowder, or any other household item. In Virginia tobacco became the chief surplus crop that was marketed in England in ever larger quantities. By 1650, Virginians could sell as much tobacco as they could raise. Perhaps the first generation of Pew pioneers saw the opportunity and learned to produce tobacco for English markets.

In Virginia the Pews prospered and multiplied. But the frontier that steadily moved westward was calling the pioneers to new adventure and conquest. When during the Revolution West Virginia opened up, members of the Pew family were among the early frontiersmen. The French and Indian War had settled the century-old contest between the French and English over control of the region. However, the struggle with the Indians continued despite the fact that, in 1774, General Andrew Lewis had defeated the allied Indian nations under Chief Cornstalk in a battle at Point Pleasant. Soon thereafter Scotch-Irish and German pioneers were moving in from Pennsylvania and Maryland, and some restless Virginians from the East. And like their ancestors at Jamestown 130 years earlier they faced hazardous Indian raids and massacres. Especially during the American Revolution the settlers suffered numerous attacks by British-led Indian armies. It was not until the turn of the century that West Virginians had grown in strength sufficient to fight off raiding parties.

But by that time two Pew boys had already moved on to another frontier. One helped to found the "village of Pittsburgh," the other settled further north in Mercer, Pennsylvania. It was this branch of the Pew family that a few decades later was to give the country some of the great pioneers of a new industry, gas and oil.

John Pew—the grandfather of the founder of Sun Oil Company, Joseph Newton Pew—came to Mercer in 1797 as one of the first eleven settlers in the region. The Indian wars had just come to an end (1795) and a wave of immigrants was about to enter Western Pennsylvania. Many came to claim land which the Commonwealth of Pennsylvania had granted them as veterans of the Revolutionary War. According to a 1780 Act of the Pennsylvania Assembly, every private was entitled to 200 acres, higher ranks receiving more. Of course, most veterans living in the east sold their claims for very little or bartered them off. Other immigrants bought a Commonwealth warrant for a tract of 100 to 400 acres and then, in order to earn the deed to the land, settled on it for five years. Or, they settled on vacant land for five years and then directly acquired the deed from the Commonwealth. Still others acquired their land from "land jobbers" who by various devices had obtained several warrants. But since the land had to be cleared, fenced and cultivated the jobber needed the settler with whom he would later divide the land upon receipt of the title. The jobber-warrantee usually kept 250 acres, the settler got 150.[1]

John Pew probably used this latter method. Born in 1769 he obviously was too young to be a veteran of the Revolution. And it is unlikely that as a young pioneer from West Virginia he traveled first to Harrisburg in order to seek a warrant to settle at the frontier. Records show that some of the land he occupied belonged to a warrantee who, in 1803, when the county of Mercer was founded, donated it to the new county.[2]

---

[1]Q. A. Gordon, "Original Land Titles in Mercer," Greenville, Pa. *Record-Argus*, 12/6/27.

[2]J. G. White, *History of Mercer County, Pennsylvania*, The Lewis Publishing Co., Chicago, 1909, p. 19.

The first Mercer court house was erected on the site in 1807.

Life at the frontier hinged around a large family. The constant danger to life and property and the never-ending chores around the house and barn made the pioneer woman equal with man. Ideally, husband and wife were one in honor and affection, and their children a common bond of love and survival. John Pew and his wife Elizabeth Vaughn, who probably stemmed from Washington County on the West Virginia border, arrived with four children. Eleven more were born to them in Mercer. The Pews were a deeply religious family as the Biblical names of the children clearly indicate. There was Samuel, Abraham, John, William, Mary, Hannah, David, Lydia, Thomas, Joseph, Elizabeth, James, Amelia, Nancy and Rebecca. Two of these died in infancy.

The Mercer pioneer was a farmer and homemaker. With the axe as his principal tool he cleared the dense forests by felling or deadening trees. Once the trees had been killed, storms would uproot them in a few years. The pioneer then would gather them in large "log heaps" and burn them. He cleared the hills first as bottom lands were too damp and vegetation too dense. His crops consisted mainly of corn, rye, and potatoes.

A big occasion in the life of a pioneer was the "raising" of his cabin. For weeks he would cut suitable trees, hew the timber, draw the hewn logs to the cabin site and then, with the help of other pioneers, his "neighbors," raise the cabin in a day. A large house—we must assume that the Pews needed a large house for their 13 children—was some 15 x 30 feet in dimension, with two rooms below and one or two in the loft. The first story usually was 9 to 10 feet high, the loft no more than 5 feet. Glass windows were unknown at the frontier, the cabin being dimly lighted through windows covered with greased paper. The ground floor consisted of clay; roof and loft floor were made of simple clapboard. The cabin door was hung on wooden hinges and latched on the inside by a short board. The few pieces of furniture that filled the cabin were homemade.[3]

The Pews of Mercer were a deeply religious family and devout Presbyterian church members. A family of 13 children makes friends easily. For pioneers friendship doubled joy and happiness, and shared the hardships and dangers of life at the frontier. The Pews even befriended the Indians who continued to roam the countryside. According to J. G. White, the squaw of Indian Chief Petty frequently visited Mrs. Pew in order to learn English. But most Indians "had no desire to learn more than enough to aid them in procuring tobacco, whiskey, etc. from the whites."[4]

During the War of 1812 the two eldest Pew boys, Samuel and Abraham, saw active duty in the "Mercer Light Infantry" and "Mercer Blues." With 94 other men they marched down to Pittsburgh and joined General Crook's brigade which, after a long march through Ohio, reinforced Gail Harrison's army on the "Maumee." According to Abraham Pew's own report, the army "did good service against the British and Indians." All men of his company returned safe and sound.[5]

Their brother John (born in 1800) was too young to march with his elder brothers. In 1823 he settled on a spread two miles south of Mercer. Soon thereafter he married Nancy Glenn with whom he raised 10 children—Samuel G., Robert, Thomas, Sarah, Jacob, Samuel, James G., John, Joseph N., Elizabeth. Joseph Newton was the youngest boy, born on July 25, 1848. If it is true that the future destiny of a child is always the work of the mother, then Nancy Glenn deserves our admiration for having raised a pioneer among pioneers, Joseph Newton, the founder of Sun Oil.

Children generally want to be busy. Therefore a wise par-

[3]*Ibid.* pp. 26-32.
[4]*History of Mercer County*, L. H. Everts & Co., Philadelphia, 1877, p. 47.
[5]*Ibid.*, p. 104.

ent takes care that their busy humor is constantly employed
in something that is of use to them and the family. On the
Pew farm there were always chores for everyone, even the
youngest members. There were potatoes to be planted, water
to be drawn, fences to be mended, eggs to be gathered, cows
to be milked, weeds to be hoed. And from the time they
were old enough, rain or shine, winter or spring, the children
walked the two miles to school in Mercer and back each day.

By the middle of the 19th century Pennsylvania had a public school system that was universal and open to all. Following the example of Massachusetts, Pennsylvania in 1834 had
required the local districts to tax themselves for public education that was to impart a common language and the values of
U.S. citizenship. In earlier years the Commonwealth had
created a number of "academies" that were to impart writing, reading and arithmetic. The Mercer Academy was established by an 1811 act of the Pennsylvania legislature and inaugurated in 1824. But long before a public school system
came into existence Mercer had three private schools that
were open to the pioneer children. Church ministers usually
supplemented their meager incomes through teaching and
tutoring. Or, a settler interested in his children's education
would invite a teacher to room and board with him. Or, several settlers would join in sponsoring a teacher for all their
children, so that no one really interested in education would
go without it.

On the Pew farm education was regarded as essential development of a sense of right, duty and honor, and as
learning to apply individual powers in the right way. There
was no future on a 200-acre dirt farm for ten children. Therefore a good education was to prepare them for other voca-
tions and occupations. They attended private schools and the
Mercer Academy until they felt ready for life. In fact, young
Joseph Newton liked school so much and did so well that, at
18, he was asked to teach in a one-room school in the tiny

community of London, Pennsylvania, a few miles south of Mercer. The money he earned and saved as teacher from 1866 to 1869 then permitted him to attend Edinboro, Pennsylvania, Normal School for one year. Thus prepared, Joseph Newton turned his attention to business.

Throughout Newton's life his father had been trading real estate with varying success. It cannot be surprising, therefore, that the son, at 22, opened a real estate business in Mercer. But there was not much life in Mercer in 1870 with barely more than 1500 inhabitants. Therefore, young Pew soon moved to a place not far away where real estate was booming. This was Titusville, originally a small lumbering town, which became the scene of feverish activity following the discovery of oil along the banks of Pithole Creek in 1859. Here Joseph Newton set himself up in the real estate business adding the services of insurance and loans for his customers. In a rapidly changing environment the opportunities for success are numerous. It is the mark of an entrepreneur that he quickly perceives the opportunities to render valuable services and thus earn profits. Young Joseph Newton was a budding entrepreneur who, in a few years, succeeded in amassing a personal fortune of some $40,000. He also won the hand of Mary Catherine Anderson, whose family was eminent in politics and law. One of her ancestors had been an aide to George Washington during his winter ordeal at Valley Forge.

Few entrepreneurs who are destined to found large enterprises manage to succeed without first suffering disappointment and misfortune. By struggling with misfortune little minds are tamed and subdued, but great men rise above it. They may receive some wounds in the adversity, but finally emerge with greater strength and better judgment. Their most valuable lessons are not learned through success, but through misadventure. And Joseph Newton Pew was no exception. Shortly after his marriage, in December 1874, he ran into serious financial trouble. He invested heavily in

"pipe-line certificates," which, in effect, were warehouse receipts for oil. But the issuers had sold several times more certificates than they actually had oil in storage. Pew lost his
savings and incurred $20,000 in debt. According to his friend,
Dr. Isaac C. Ketler, founder and president of Grove City College, "following his reverses, Mr. Pew almost immediately
tried his fortune in the Parker's Landing and Bullion Oil
Fields and, not being very successful, removed in 1876, to
Bradford, Pennsylvania, where he was prosperous in his oil
operations and especially in an original enterprise of piping
natural gas for domestic uses into the town of Olean, New
York."[6]

Joseph Newton's remarkable stamina in the face of adversity and his great honesty towards his creditors provided a
natural attraction to a Titusville banker, Edward O. Emerson,
who in a similar misfortune in the banking business had re-
paid every penny of his depositors' money. In 1876, Mr. Pew
and Mr. Emerson entered into a partnership and launched a
natural gas business in Bradford, Pennsylvania and later
Olean, New York.

McKean County in which Bradford is located was one of
the last frontier counties of the state. It was covered with
thick pine forests which made lumbering the chief attraction
for new settlers. In 1875 oil was discovered, and thousands
of people—drillers, speculators, teamsters, merchants and
laborers came to Bradford to seek their fortunes. There was
opportunity for the new partnership—Joseph Newton Pew at
the age of 28 and Edward O. Emerson at 42. The young Pew
family moved to Bradford to work hard at the business Newton already knew a great deal about. The first project was to
pipe natural gas to drilling sites in the Bradford oil fields.
Cheaper than coal, gas proved to be an excellent fuel for
heating boilers of drilling rigs and pumping oil wells. The

---

[6]*Our Sun*, Special 75th Anniversary Issue, 1961, p. 12.

venture succeeded so well that on February 1, 1881, the partners incorporated and formed the Keystone Gas Company. It supplied gas not only to the oil field but also for heat and light to residents of Bradford. Within a short time, Keystone extended its operations to provide natural gas to Olean, New York, 30 miles to the north.

The social life in Bradford centered around the church. The Pew family held daily morning worship in the home and faithfully attended church on Sundays. There were few cultural events, but occasionally a circus came to town. And in the late summer a county fair with its exhibits and prizes, and sometimes horse races, provided diversion and entertainment. At the end of the harvest season the community met for a picnic. All work was put aside on that day and hundreds of people drove wagons, buggies and surreys to the picnic grounds.[7]

Happy is the family where the parents reign with affection and the children submit in love. Already in Bradford the Pew family evidenced an exceptional degree of family affinity that was to characterize the Pews for the next one hundred years. It was to make a job with Sun Oil Company a traditional occupation for Pews. In fact, at one time or another most descendants of both Joseph Newton and his elder brother Thomas worked for Sun Oil or one of its subsidiaries. Robert C. Pew was the first nephew of Joseph Newton who, at 18, joined his uncle at Bradford to begin an apprenticeship in the oil and gas business under his uncle's tutelage. He proved himself such an able and trustworthy assistant that just short of his 23rd birthday he became a partner in the company.

On January 27, 1882, the Pew family was blessed by the birth of their second child, John Howard. For six lonely years when Joseph Newton labored hard from dawn to dusk in the

---

[7]John W. Ray, *History of Western Pennsylvania*, Riverside Press of Athens, Pa., 1941, p. 357.

oil fields of Bradford young Arthur had been his mother's only companion. Now he was joined by a younger brother who was destined to guide and direct the family business after his father's death in 1912.

The year 1882 is not known for any particular milestone in American history. Chester A. Arthur had just become President after James B. Garfield was assassinated by a disgruntled office-seeker. The population of the United States numbered approximately 53 million and was growing rapidly due to high birthrates and massive immigration from Western and Central Europe. The year marked the construction of the first hydro-electric plant in Appleton, Wisconsin, and the first use of incandescent light bulbs in homes and offices. The year also saw the formation of the Standard Oil Trust, which made John D. Rockefeller and his associates "trustees" of several oil companies. For decades to come this Trust was the main competitor to the fledgling enterprise of Messrs. Emerson and Pew. But their eminent success in competition with the Standard Oil Trust was to disprove cogently the popular notion of the Trust's monopolistic position within the oil industry.

During the decade of the 1880's America remained the land of opportunity not only for all Americans but also for millions of poor European migrants and well-to-do-investors. The country was recovering from the doubts and divisions of the Civil War and regaining its self-confidence and social stability. There was a remarkable uniformity in fundamental economic and social beliefs although the political system was shaped and maintained by two opposing political parties. But both parties were trying to capture the same middle-class vote by saying the same thing in two different ways. The Republican Party denied any conflict between public welfare and individualism. It considered itself the party of the small entrepreneur, the hard-working farmer and the decent worker. Supported by most intellectuals, it combined idealism with enthusiasm for the private property order. The Democratic Party enjoyed a majority in the House of Representatives for nine of the eighteen congresses between 1865 and 1901. Its stronghold was the South where the Republican party was practically extinct. In the North it enjoyed strength and support in the cities among minorities, poor workers and immigrants. Some intellectual support came from a small number of wealthy bankers and international traders who abhorred the protectionist bias of the Republicans. But in spite of much squabbling about trivia that passed as real political problems, the American utopia for Republicans and Democrats alike remained capitalist America.

Two great conflicts nevertheless aroused the emotions of many Americans: the reconstruction of the South and the populist movement in the North. Reconstruction involved, among other things, the position of the Negro in American political, social and economic life, which proved to be a painful and insoluble issue then and for many decades to come. The populist movement drew together all the strands of malcontent, and rose to challenge the capitalist philosophy of the age. It proposed a graduated income tax, government ownership of railroads, restriction of immigration in the interests of labor, and above all, a policy of easy money and credit through unlimited coinage of silver. It arrayed agriculture against industry, farmers against bankers and railroad men, the poor against the rich, labor against capital. Populism, in fact, anticipated some of the characteristics of later liberalism and many economic and social policies of the twentieth century.[8]

The Pews of Bradford were Republicans like most small businessmen in the North. The Republican respect for the dynamic economic forces of the age and unqualified oppo-

---

[8]Cr. *The New Cambridge Modern History,* Volume XI, Material Progress and World-wide Problems, 1870-1898, Cambridge, the University Press, 1962, pp. 487-515.

sition to slavery, which had given birth to the Republican Party, appealed to the Pews. But the oil and gas business, which was small but profitable in Bradford, consumed all their time and strength. In fact, the success led Messrs. Emerson and Pew, in 1882, to purchase leases nearby the giant Haymaker gas well at Murrysville, near Pittsburgh. After Bradford and Olean, Pittsburgh now loomed as an exciting market for a new venture and a new company, the Penn Fuel Company.

Pittsburgh during the 1880's was a unique center of industry. For several decades it had been the natural gateway to the West. Now it was alive with new industry and commerce and gaining rapidly in industrial importance. Its strategic location at the confluence of two navigable rivers, the Monongahela and the Allegheny forming the Ohio River, makes it a leading transportation center. And its natural resources such as abundant timber, clay for bricks, sand for glass, petroleum, natural gas and coal, and a plentiful supply of water for industrial uses, were inviting American industry to locate in Pittsburgh. In addition, a young population with a high percentage of new immigrants who were eager to work long and hard gave Pittsburgh early dominance in such industries as steel, electric power and aluminum. But no discussion of the industrial growth of Pittsburgh would be complete without mention of the great contributions by such industrial giants as Andrew Carnegie and George Westinghouse.

When Joseph Newton Pew arrived in 1882, Pittsburgh had a population of 235,000. The city was growing by leaps and bounds; but few Pittsburghers realized that they were in need of natural gas. The Penn Fuel Company of Messrs. Emerson and Pew immediately embarked upon correcting this apparent oversight by building gas pipe lines to the city. Pittsburgh thus became the first major city in the U.S. that was supplied with natural gas for home and industrial use.

To market a new service or product takes drive, imagination, ingenuity, and persuasion. Man is naturally reluctant to make changes and try innovations. But in industry the competition of the pace setters who have the vision and knowledge of the new product tends to force all others to follow suit lest they be eliminated through financial losses and failure. This is why Joseph Newton tried hard to market his gas in the Carnegie Steel mills. He went to Andrew Carnegie and offered to supply his mills with gas "free of charge." Finally convinced of the economic advantages of gas Carnegie consented to take it, but proudly retorted, "I'll pay for it."

After two years of hectic commuting between Bradford and Pittsburgh Joseph Newton moved his family to North Highland Avenue in Pittsburgh. Soon thereafter young Arthur and John Howard were joined by two sisters and a brother, Mary Ethel, Joseph Newton Jr., and Mabel Anderson. The change from a frontier community to a growing metropolitan area was a welcome one for Mary and Newton Pew. There were plays, operettas, shops, parties and an occasional bridge game. And now that he was closer to his parental home in Mercer, Joseph Newton visited it frequently with his family. In 1885 he purchased the homestead from his older brother and began to improve the house and round out his land holdings. Throughout their lives the children recalled spending very pleasurable summers "in the country."

Pittsburgh was an interesting town in which to grow up. But the quality of life did not change very much for the Pew family no matter where they lived. For it was a closely-knit family, always doing things together. They joined the East Liberty Presbyterian Church and Howard was later to say, "My father saw to it that I never missed attending Sunday School and church." School was very important for the children and they all were rather good students. All attended the best private schools around Pittsburgh and later Philadelphia. Joe and Ethel first went to the Alinda, Ethel then to Miss Thurston's School and Joe to Shady Side Academy. He followed Arthur and Howard who also attended the Academy in preparation for college. Mabel went to Miss Thurston's and later Miss Wright's at Bryn Mawr. Arthur earned a degree at Princeton, Howard at Grove City College, Joseph at Cornell, and Ethel at Bryn Mawr.

The aim of their education was to teach them how to think rather than what to think—to improve their minds so as to enable them to think for themselves. Good education develops a sense of right, duty and honor. And good business rests on these qualities as well as sound judgment. While the Pew children were busily training their minds and building habits, hopes, and faiths, their father continued to build the gas business. When some Pittsburgh investors made an attractive offer to buy the Penn Fuel Company, Messrs. Emerson and Pew readily sold out. But as an indication of their indomitable energy and entrepreneurial drive they immediately formed a new company, The Peoples Natural Gas Company, which continues today to serve the people of Pittsburgh and Western Pennsylvania, 89 years later.

Before the new enterprise was fully operative the discovery of oil and gas near Lima, Ohio, attracted their attention. Early in 1886 they sent Robert C. Pew to scout the possibility of securing leases, and on his recommendation, acquired two leases for oil exploration, drilling and production. While at first this was considered an interesting investment and a sideline operation, it grew until it overshadowed the western Pennsylvania business. With its pipe lines, leases, storage tanks and tank cars the company quickly emerged as one of Ohio's leading suppliers of crude. When the operations became very substantial the partners incorporated an independent company, the Sun Oil Line Company. And after more acquisitions the scattered operations were incorporated in 1890 into the Sun Oil Company (Ohio) for the purpose of "producing petroleum, rock and carbon oil; transporting and storing same; refining, purifying, manufacturing, shipping, selling and marketing such oil and its various products. . . ."[9] Finally, four years later, the partners together with a Cleveland company formed the Diamond Oil Company to buy what is now the Company's Toledo Refinery. Thus Messrs. Pew and Emerson were well on their way to create a fully integrated organization.

By the close of the century Joseph Newton Pew began to consider leaving the natural gas business and devoting his time and effort exclusively to petroleum operations. In later years Howard was to say, "My father taught me not to diversify my efforts, but to put all my eggs in one basket and take a firm grip on the handle." Apparently Newton was doing just this by selling Peoples Gas to Standard Oil and buying out Edward Emerson's interest in the Sun Oil Company. From then until his death, in 1912, Joseph Newton Pew was at the helm of a rapidly growing organization whose various branches and parts were managed by an increasing number of his nephews and children.

J. Howard was still in college when his father bought out E. O. Emerson, his partner for 23 years (from 1876 to 1899). Howard was in his junior year at Grove City College, working towards a Bachelor of Science degree. It seemed natural for him to be at this institution where his father was Chairman of the Board. "I hardly remember a time when I did not know Grove City College," J. Howard was to say later.[10] He fondly remembered his visits to the campus as a boy where he enjoyed climbing over beams and rafters of a building under construction. The moment he felt Shady Side Academy had sufficiently prepared him, he enrolled at the College.

In 1895 Grove City College, under the able leadership of its president and founder, Dr. Isaac C. Ketler, had undergone a reorganization. It had changed from a privately owned com-

---

[9]*Our Sun*, 75th Anniversary Issue, 1961, p. 18.
[10]Speech at Founders' Day Assembly, April 11, 1951, p. 2.

pany whose stock was held by local residents and parents of
students to a "public charity," a non-profit educational institution controlled by a self-perpetuating board of trustees.
And this Board had elected an eminent businessman, Joseph
Newton Pew of Pittsburgh, its president. The College's President, Dr. Ketler, had been a student of Joseph Newton some
27 years earlier when the latter was a young teacher in a one-
room school at London. Later, when his gas business in Bradford became successful, Pew had asked his former student,
whose exceptional abilities he well remembered, to join him
in his growing enterprise. But Mr. Ketler had declined since
his interests were pointing him in another direction—towards
higher education. Now, many years later, Mr. Pew was to join
Dr. Ketler in the management of a young educational institution. For Joseph Newton the College was to become his
main philanthropy which, after his death, was carried on with
great dedication by his children.

To J. Howard, Grove City College afforded a wide range of
subjects in the natural sciences. It provided excellent instruction in such fields as physiology, geography, physics, chem-
istry, zoology, botany, biology, astronomy and geology. In addition, Howard received instruction in the liberal arts, such as
English, Latin, German, mathematics, history, philosophy,
metaphysics, political science and international law. Since
Grove City College prided itself in being a nondenomina-
tional Christian college Howard, in his junior year, also was
taking a Bible course. And, like every other male student at
the College, he was occupied for five hours each week with
instruction and training in the Military Department, which
later was to become the Reserve Officer Training Corps
(ROTC). For his proficiency in his military duties he earned
the rank of corporal.

In those years the College lacked the splendid dormitory
facilities it was to build many years later. Most students
roomed in private homes in town for which they paid a going

rate of $7.50 per term, plus 40 to 60 cents per week for cooking privileges. Good boarding in a private family, everything furnished, was available at $2.50 to $3.00 per week. And total expenses for a college year consisting of three terms were estimated at $150 per year. However, the expenses of J. Howard and many other students who could afford their own transportation, that is, horse and buggy, were slightly higher. The horse and buggy permitted him over weekends, to visit the Pew homestead 7 miles to the north in Mercer, or to return home to Pittsburgh 60 miles to the south. But occasionally Howard would ride his bicycle to Pittsburgh which, in later years, afforded him satisfaction and pride that he could make the trip in a day.

Howard graduated from Grove City College in 1900, at the age of 18. Whenever he was complimented for this scholastic achievement he would talk about all the summer schools he attended, and add with a smile: "I didn't like school, after all." Angeline Stewart, a classmate of Howard's remembered him as a rather shy and quiet boy who didn't play any sports or participate in any extracurricular activities. He didn't even have a girl friend. It was her explanation that he was so much younger than his classmates.

After graduation from Grove City College, J. Howard took some graduate courses at Massachusetts Institute of Technology which had already gained a nation-wide reputation for engineering and the sciences. But while he was listening to lectures on thermodynamics and structural design, his mind often wandered to the hustle and bustle of the Sun Oil fields in Ohio and to the new frontier of science and industry. It was calling him as the old frontier had beckoned his ancestors.

Sun Oil Company was about to embark upon a new venture that was most exciting and challenging. Spindletop, up to that time the largest known oil field in the world, had been discovered near Beaumont, Texas, in January of 1901.

Joseph Newton immediately sent his trusted nephew, Robert, to appraise the field. When Joseph Newton heard the report, he ordered with astute foresight that the cheap crude oil be bought as quickly as transportation and storage facilities could be developed. With characteristic vision he proposed to ship the oil to the east by tanker and build a refinery near Philadelphia that would process the Texas crude. For this purpose he incorporated the Sun Company of New Jersey, on May 2, 1901, and approached a major customer of the products of his Toledo Refinery, the United Gas Improvement Company of Philadelphia, to finance the project. The latter promptly subscribed to 45 per cent of Sun Company's stock; Joseph Newton and his associates kept the balance. By the end of the year construction of the new refinery had already begun on the Delaware River at Marcus Hook, Pennsylvania. Joseph Newton's oldest son, Arthur, was appointed vice president, and J. Howard was to start his career in the oil business as development engineer.

For the first eleven years of his working life, Howard's headquarters were in Marcus Hook. Most of that time both his office and living quarters were at the old office building across the railroad from Number One Boiler House. Here he learned to work, and learned what it meant to earn his own living. Here he studied crude oil, how it was refined, packaged and shipped. But above all, he learned to understand and work with men, and appreciate the loyalty and support of the men working in the plant—men to whom long hours and hard work were of slight concern compared to their desire to make the business a success.[11]

As development engineer J. Howard was assigned the task of converting the black residue from refined Texas crude into a more profitable product than the industrial fuel for

---

[11]J. Howard Pew, *Your Company's Problems are Your Problems*, address to Employees Athletic Assn. of the Sun Oil Co. at the dedication of their new recreation property, Marcus Hook, Pa., September 26, 1936.

which it was commonly used. More and more of this residue accumulated in the storage tanks while Howard and his crew experimented and tested, failed and tried again. Their efforts were finally rewarded when they discovered an excellent lubricant that could be used by itself or added to other lubricants. Marketed as Sun Red Stock, it won worldwide acclaim and proved to be one of the most profitable items produced by the company at that time. In 1904 he developed a process by which a high-quality asphalt was produced—the first commercially successful petroleum asphalt. It became Sun's first trademarked item called Hydrolene. Thus, to his great joy and satisfaction, Howard was substantially contributing to the success of Sun Oil Company.

There were pleasures mixed with hard work. In the summer of 1903 Joseph Newton decided to take his whole family to Europe. While the father attended to business, his family enjoyed visiting historic places and meeting foreign people. They returned the richer for having visited the old countries and more appreciative of their own. It was their only trip together, for from that year on until his death Joseph Newton made a business trip to Europe every summer taking only his two daughters along. In 1904 the family moved from Pittsburgh to Philadelphia to the Tony Biddle house on Walnut Street. And a year later Joseph Newton bought a beautiful house on Morris Avenue in Bryn Mawr, and named it "Glenmede" in honor of his mother, Nancy Glenn. The new house was to become the scene of lively social life, especially for 21-year-old Ethel and 16-year-old Mabel.

It was at one of the parties to which Ethel had invited her friend, the beautiful Helen Thompson of Pittsburgh, that Howard met his future wife. When Ethel introduced Miss Thompson to her brother he showed immediate interest in this thoughtful and kind young woman. For Howard, who was basically shy and reserved, her outgoing personality was most attractive, and her genuine curiosity about many things

provided the communication that was needed for friendship to
flower. After a two-year courtship they were married (1907)
and went to Europe on a wedding trip. Mrs. Pew merrily told
later that her father, a successful Pittsburgh businessman,
noted with approval that Howard could drive a car, which
would enable his son-in-law to drive a truck in case the oil
business would fail. When they realized that they would have
no natural children they adopted three—Roberta, George, and
Frances, in that order. Frances described him as "A very
wonderful daddy, but an austere father." While he was not
indulging his children he gave them many things, such as a
horse to ride, lessons in music and dancing, tickets to con-
certs, and an ample allowance. But above all, he was there
when they needed to talk and air their problems. Howard and
Helen remained a very devoted couple throughout 57 years
of wedlock. When, in 1950, Mrs. Pew fell seriously ill with a
rare blood disease, Howard stayed with her constantly and
worked diligently with doctors and blood specialists to find a
cure. He contributed in large measure to the treatment
that restored her to health.

His years as superintendent of the Marcus Hook Refinery
were some of the happiest of his life. He broadened his knowledge about every phase of the oil business. He even learned
how to handle unruly crews when some men had imbibed too
freely. It is told that on such occasions he would go to the
local priest for assistance. It evidently was very effective, for
later he merely needed to mention the priest to get his men
back to work. With Howard in charge of research and refining, the Company's line of products thus continued to grow—
by 1910 more than 100 products carried Sun's trade name.

But this happy period of youthful building was about to end.
On October 10, 1912, Joseph Newton Pew suffered a fatal
heart attack in his office. Thus, at 64, the life of the founder
of Sun Oil had ended. If genius is the spirit of discovery, being
in advance of its time, the pioneer for the generation to come,

then Joseph Newton surely was a genius. Henry Wadsworth Longfellow could have said of him:

> All the means of action—the shapeless masses—the materials— lie everywhere about us. What we need is the celestial fire to change the flint into the transparent crystal, bright and clear. That fire is genius.

The Sun Company was an enterprise of which Joseph Newton was justifiably proud. But how would his children carry on the difficult task? In his will Joseph Newton had directed that his stock be placed in trust for his family for a period of 20 years. But there was no hesitancy on the part of his heirs to continue to manage and build the company. In less than two weeks after his father's death 30-year-old John Howard was elected president by his family. His younger brother, Joseph Newton, Jr., was made vice president. With Joseph as the adventuresome member and Howard as the restrained one, more nearly like his father, they became an excellent management team. Throughout the years they were great friends, frequently visiting each others' offices, sharing all of their successes and commiserating over failures.

With automobiles now being mass-produced and airplanes in the fledgling stage the demand for Sun's products was growing continuously. Although Howard, as president, now worked in the Philadelphia company office, he made weekly trips to Marcus Hook. He spent many hours with his men seeking their ideas and suggestions for improving the company products or for reducing operating costs so that the business would continue to grow. In 1915, while World War I was raging in Europe, Sun's extensive marketing operations necesitated Howard's visit to England. On a side trip to Germany he was shown some submarine construction which led him to the conviction that Sun Company should build ships or tankers of their own in order to assure world-wide distribution of Sun Company's products. With the proceeds of an unfurnished tanker that was being built for Sun they hastily began constructing their own shipyard at Chester, Pennsylvania. It was completed in record time and the Sun Shipbuilding Company opened in May, 1916 and launched its first vessel, the S.S. *Chester Sun* on October 30, 1917. By 1918 some 10,000 men were building 10,000-ton tankers at the rate of 1 per month.

The story of the Sun Shipbuilding Company is a saga of extraordinary vision and determination. With Howard as president of Sun Oil Company and his younger brother Joe in charge of the shipyard, the Sun operation was to become the largest yard in the world. In World War II it contributed probably more to the success of American armies overseas than any other industrial effort. German submarines were striking terrible blows at the most vital arteries of the United States and its Allies by sinking some 3,100,000 tons of tankers in 1942 alone, tankers loaded with aviation fuel, gasoline to operate our divisions of tanks and artillery, fuel oil for the Naval and Merchant Marine fleets. But the shipbuilders of America, with Sun Ship leading the effort, thwarted the German strategy. For every ton sunk, a new ton went to sea. The Sun Shipbuilding Company built 250 major vessels during the war. It repaired 1200 ships in its dry docks. In 1942 it built two-thirds of all new tankers in this country, in 1943, at the peak of the war effort, one half; and later, when new shipyards came into operation, a declining percentage. For the entire period of the war Sun Ship constructed 40 per cent of all tankers built. In fact, it built more ships than the entire British Empire was able to construct. And Sun Ship was building a sturdier, larger and faster tanker than it was constructing before the war. The full extent of the contribution which Sun Ship has made to winning the war can only be surmised.

The rapid expansion of the company during World War I was not without great risk. Heavy financial commitments place the solvency of an enterprise in jeopardy if current production does not yield the revenue needed to meet the commitments. This is probably the reason the partners of the United Gas Improvement Company, who held 45 per cent of the Company stock, felt rather uneasy about that young Pew management. After all, when the U.S. entered World War I, Howard, the President, was merely 35 and Joe, the shipbuilder, only 30. Being aware of the fears and misgivings of their U.G.I. partners the Pews offered to buy them out. Agreement was quickly reached, and the transaction was completed in January, 1918.

Sun Company came out of the war much stronger than it was in 1914 with its primary interest in lubricating and industrial oils. But it was becoming clearer all along that petroleum's once-useless by-product, gasoline, was now really big business. Never to be left behind, the partners decided to produce Sunoco Motor Oil and gasoline for commercial use, and to begin marketing them in their own service stations in Toledo, Ohio, and Ardmore, Pennsylvania. In keeping with this new policy, the Company's charter was amended to change its name to Sun Oil Company in 1922.

An important factor in the phenomenal success of Sun Oil was Howard's exceptional ability in selecting capable executives and motivating his men. He wisely used what is probably the strongest motivation of all: the pride and joy of ownership. Therefore, Sun Oil became probably the first American company of substantial size that instituted a stock purchase plan for employees in 1926. In preparation for this momentous policy the Company needed to go public. It was an historic moment when, on November 12, 1925, Sun Oil stock appeared for the first time on Wall Street's big board.

At a time when radical social and economic thought was spreading rapidly, demanding that all facilities of production be nationalized or, at least, be controlled by government, when labor demagogues were busily arousing the workers' suspicion and hatred of their employers, "the capitalists," J. Howard Pew was fighting back. He clearly saw long before many fellow industrialists that the future of the private property system was at stake, as well as the profitability of his own enterprise. To defend the system with its individual initiative, incentive, ingenuity and resourcefulness, he introduced a stock purchase plan for employees that has been singularly effective ideologically and economically. It provided many millions of dollars in individual savings for company growth and expansion. And it administered a powerful antidote to economic radicalism that is so detrimental to productivity.

After one year of employment the stock purchase plan offers all employees the opportunity to accumulate important wealth with a modest investment. If an employee entered the Plan at its beginning in 1926, and receiving just 10 shares in each distribution, he owned, at the time of Mr. Pew's death, 410 shares of which only 192 were purchased with his own money. With the stock dividends which Sun Oil frequently declared these shares grew to 2,884 shares worth $145,281.50. But this is not all. Over the years the same employee received cash dividends amounting to $32,061 in addition to a great many fractional shares worth several thousand dollars. Altogether employees acquired a cumulative total of 4,701,712 shares worth considerably more than $200 million. By mid-1971 Sun stockholder records showed that 7,739 of some 40,000 stockholders were employees, or close to 20 per cent.

Few industrialists, if any, have shown such a consistent concern for their employees, as did J. Howard Pew. The motto of his concern was also his motto of wisdom.

The greatest test of his genuine interest in the well-being of his employees probably came during the Great Depression. Like other business and industry, Sun Oil Company was hit hard. Gross operating revenue sank from $98 million in 1930 to $69 million in 1931 and $67 million in 1932; net income slid from $7.75 million to $3.1 million and $4.2 million respectively. But management never lost faith in the initiative and industriousness of its employees and decided to forge ahead because, as Howard stated in the 1931 Annual Report, the Company believed "this to be an opportune time to complete its building and improvement program." This program included building the multi-million-dollar pipeline from the Marcus Hook Refinery to Cleveland and on to Syracuse. Under the supervision of J. N. Pew, Jr. this pipeline was one of the first built for moving refined products to marketing areas. An investment of $9.5 million was made to modernize the tanker fleet; the Marcus Hook Refinery was enlarged; the Sun-Yount-Lee crude pipeline was constructed in Texas; the products pipeline was extended from Twin Oaks, Pennsylvania to Newark, New Jersey. In addition to this bold leadership in initiating new projects, Sun Oil—unlike its competitors—refused to make general lay-offs or wage reductions. At a conference with most of the officers in the President's office when the financial reports for the first quarter of 1932 were discussed, Howard finally instructed one of his associates to telephone all company offices with the following message: "There will be no reduction in salaries nor rates of pay throughout the company—please impress upon everyone to help make the second half better than the first half." The management still treated its employees, though now numbering 12,000, as though it were a large family. The employees loyally responded with renewed effort and efficiency.

It would be possible to relate countless examples of his great concern and love of man. Deeply rooted in his religion, this love was flowing from his image of God and was his essence of brotherly love. When an explosion at the Marcus Hook Refinery injured and hospitalized several men, Howard visited them each morning for five or six weeks. He would take books and magazines to them; and when they needed skin grafts, he engaged the best specialist for the operation.

When, after World War II, the U.S. Government imposed

stringent quotas on the importation of crude oil from abroad,
all other companies retired many tankers from service and
dismissed thousands of sailors. Equally affected but genuine-
ly concerned about the well-being of its employees, Sun Oil
Company continued to run all its tankers with smaller loads.
Only when the number of sailors had declined sufficiently
through natural attrition were Sun Oil tankers withdrawn
from service. When the employees expressed their gratitude
and appreciation for this "uneconomic" and yet so human
operation, J. Howard cherished the letter. He framed it and
displayed it on the wall of his office.

He never would do business with anyone or any company
whose honesty was in doubt. He preferred a loss before unjust gain by dealing with unscrupulous operators. After all, a
loss brings grief but once, an unjust gain forever. At one time
Sun Oil had an opportunity to go into business with a big
Mexican promoter who promised inordinate gains. While
other executives were intrigued by the prospect of large profits, Mr. Pew rejected the deal: "It doesn't make any difference
how much money is involved—I won't deal with anyone I
think is dishonest." Afterwards it turned out that the promoter was indeed a fraud.

Most people knew J. Howard as a very stern and serious-
minded gentleman. But his friends were aware of his great
sense of humor. He was quick to retort to a joke or play of
words, and enjoyed reciting limericks. Grove City College
trustees recall that Mr. Pew could entertain them for hours,
rolling off an indefinite number of rhymes. He loved the
company of a bridge game, from which he frequently
emerged as the winner. In later years, when there were not
many old friends left to play, he was often the only man at the
table.

Every Wednesday afternoon Howard Pew sought recreation and exercise on the golf course. No matter who would
come to town and want to see him that afternoon, he would
play golf. "I just can't see you today," he would say on the

phone, "This is the one afternoon I have reserved for golf. You wouldn't deny an old man like me one afternoon a week, would you?" He was a slow and deliberate player who would make the shot exactly the way he wanted to make it. Occasionally he would equal or break his age, which, according to his daughter, Frances, was one of his goals in his life.

J. Howard Pew was highly disciplined in anything he undertook. This extended to his personal habits where he observed a certain time for work, certain foods to eat, certain exercises to take, a certain time for sleep. His friend, Billy Graham, was convinced that Howard's holding to this regimen sustained his remarkable health and gave him long life. Weir Ketler, his Grove City College associate, saw his great discipline as a responsibility to set an example to his many fellow workers. But Howard Pew put it this way: "It's only when you put things in retirement that they get dull. That's the mistake of men retiring too early. You should keep active. You'll live longer."

Mr. Pew had a remarkable memory until the day he died. He could long retain numerous figures and calculations, and recite lengthy poems and speeches. Architect Al Panepinto, his associate and consultant since the mid-thirties, recalls with awe how Pew would memorize the detailed costs of plumbing, heating, electricity, landscaping and furnishings of a new building, having heard them just once. Allyn Bell recalls how, at dinner parties, Mr. Pew would recite lengthy poems such as *Casey at the Bat* and many others. And anyone who ever heard him speak could not but marvel at his flawless delivery of a lengthy speech which he had easily put to memory, having dictated it first to his faithful secretary, Miss Baker. After a lengthy testimony before a Federal Commission in Washington, one of the members was so impressed by Mr. Pew's presentation and appearance that he felt compelled to comment: "Mr. Pew not only sounds like an affidavit, he looks like one!"

J. Howard Pew's achievements with Sun Oil earned him

wide acclaim as a petroleum pioneer and giant of the industry. In time, he became one of the wealthiest men in America. But in a private property system, such as ours, great wealth always consists of productive capital that produces goods and services for the people and employs thousands of men. J. Howard Pew's wealth consisted almost entirely of tankers and refineries, pipelines and service stations. His consumptive wealth was negligible indeed compared with the productive wealth that rendered services to millions of consumers. He was a great leader of men who knew how to motivate them and win their loyal cooperation. But he was also fascinated by technology to which he made remarkable contributions.

It would be difficult to enumerate the inventions and new processes of production which J. Howard Pew introduced to the industry. It is true, as the president of a large enterprise, he could no longer spend his time in the laboratory searching for new products and methods, as he had done in his younger years at Marcus Hook. But as president he brilliantly used his technological knowledge in employing new methods and directing valuable research. In 1931, his company was the first to complete a pipeline between Marcus Hook and Cleveland that moved refined products to marketing areas. But the most significant technological achievement of the 1930's was the development of catalytic cracking. The French inventor, Eugene Houdry, had tried in vain to market his process with several large American oil companies. When it finally came to the attention of J. Howard Pew, he helped the inventor to perfect it and then designed and constructed the world's first, full-scale catalytic plant which, when put on stream in 1937, produced a higher percentage of gasoline of much higher octane quality. This gasoline fueled more than half of all American army and navy planes in 1942 and 1943. All other companies later imitated his process.

Perhaps the most remarkable of his technological achievements is understood by the world only now, years after his

death. Howard Pew clearly foresaw the "energy crisis" of the
1970's and personally warned President Nixon about it. Ob-
serving the steady tightening of the noose by Federal and
state taxation, restrictions, and controls, together with a
growing American dependence on foreign oil, he launched
the first large-scale extraction of oil from Alberta's tar sands
by a new Sun subsidiary, Great Canadian Oil Sands, Ltd. The
beneficial impact of this revolutionary technique will be felt
by Americans for decades to come.

Long before noisy environmentalists discovered problems
of industrial pollution and called on government to pass restrictive laws, Howard Pew was coping with the problems. At
great expense his refineries managed to keep hydrocarbons
out of the air through the exclusive use of floating roof tanks
and pipelines connecting the tanks. For him it was the proper
thing to do. When a tornado in three hours dropped 11 inches
of rain on a refinery, causing a creek to flood Sun facilities
with three feet of water, some sulphuric sludge and oil spilled
and polluted some houses along the raging stream. Without
hesitation or delay, Sun Oil paid for the damage to the
homes.

J. Howard Pew brought to business some of the qualities
that actuate the explorer, scientist and artist: the zest, the
openmindedness, even the disinterestedness with which the
scientist explores his field of pure research. At the end of
World War I, for instance, Sun Oil products arrived in oil-
starved Germany six weeks before any other competitor appeared on the scene. During the peace negotiations at Ver-
sailles, Mr. Pew quietly assembled a fleet of tankers off Ham-
burg and Bremen. As word came from Washington that the
peace treaty had been signed his waiting tankers steamed
into the German ports. When asked how much money he
made on the deal he merely smiled and shrugged his shoulders. As always, money was not his motivation—to be the first
in service was important to him.

Fifteen years later, Mr. Pew became convinced that Hitler

was going to ruin Germany, either by internal strife or foreign war. He therefore arranged to sell Sun's interests in a German firm that was marketing Sun lubricating oils and greases. But there was foreign exchange control, a vicious government control over money exchange, that prevented withdrawal of the proceeds from Germany. While the funds of other foreign companies were frozen in blocked accounts, Mr. Pew managed to get all his money out. He bought six-inch steel pipes suitable for pipelines and had them shipped to Sun at Philadelphia. The value of the pipes matched the proceeds from the sale of his German interests.

To J. Howard Pew, every wanton restraint of individual liberty, whether practiced by a dictator or a popular government, was a degree of tyranny. He opposed every form of government intervention with the creative activity of man. With heavy heart he watched the growth of government in Washington and saw its bureaucracy encroach upon the traditional freedoms of Americans. To him central planning and control meant denial of individual freedom to plan and control. Therefore, in countless speeches, many of which were published, he pleaded the case for individual freedom and the private property order, which to him was "the great American heritage."

To Howard Pew the greatest economic evil of our time was the ever-accelerating inflation that is depriving the American people of their earned incomes and savings. He blamed irresponsible fiscal and monetary policies for the depreciation and derided the attempts of price stabilizers to halt inflation through price controls. For controls merely discourage production and cause unemployment, generate shortages and breed black markets, and otherwise disarrange the whole economic process. To alleviate an evil policy with evil means, he was convinced, cannot yield noble effects.

J. Howard Pew was president of Sun Oil Company for 35 years. Under his management the Company grew nearly forty times over. Year by year, step by step, little by little, that was his way to achievement, his way to wisdom and greatness. He asked to be relieved of his position because in his judgment a chief executive, at age 65, should make way for youth with new zest, hope and energy. Capable successors to the president are denied the opportunity to lead the company if he fails to make way. Howard Pew, therefore, surrendered his place to the Company's 37-year-old comptroller, Robert G. Dunlop. But his wisdom and knowledge continued to be felt in the management of Sun Oil Company, for he served as a member of the Board until 1963 when he assumed the chairmanship upon the death of his younger brother, Joseph, and as chairman of the executive committee from February 1970, following the Company's merger with Sunray DX Oil Company, until his death on November 27, 1971.

At sixty-five a man has passed most of the ridges and valleys of life. Excepting only death, he has no adversary left to meet. Old age increases the circle of his pains and contracts that of his pleasures. J. Howard Pew lived to be 89, and one of the pains he had to suffer was the death of all his friends and colleagues. He buried practically all of them, and half of the next generation after him. There were times when he attended at least one funeral a week. But no grief was so acute to him as the loss of first his brother, Joe, and then his beloved wife, in 1963. Although quite different in demeanor and deportment, his brother had been his business partner for 55 years. In later years as members of the Board they would visit each other frequently and spend many hours in their offices at opposite ends of the 19th floor of the Sun Oil building and have lunch together at the Racquet Club.

Soon after the death of his brother Joe, Howard lost his wife, his sole partner and sole part of all his joys. Their daughter, Frances Pew Hayes, later expressed her surprise that he had the strength to live on without her. "And yet," she would say, "I see more of my mother coming out in my father every

day. He reflects what she said and did and what she stood
for." In answer to an expression of sympathy, J. Howard Pew
wrote these words: "Mrs. Pew and I had 57 years together,
for which I am most grateful. But I realize that her time had
come, and it was best for her to pass on; but with me it leaves
a void which can never be filled. It may be presumptuous
on my part, but I must tell you that she was a truly remarkable woman. I never knew her to say an unkind word about
anyone; and I am sure she never entertained an unworthy or
mean thought."

Upon retirement from the presidency, he found more time
and strength for other important labors that needed to be
done. But he was aware that philanthropy, like charity, must
begin at home and from there extend in ever wider circles.
And true philanthropy that flows from faith in God does not
bury its gold in ostentatious giving, but plants its seed in the
human heart.

To J. Howard Pew, true religion shows its influence in
every part of man's conduct. With his great wealth and entrepreneurial ability he, therefore, sought to promote Christian education and training. He was instrumental in the
founding of a theological seminary in Boston and endeavored
to make it the leading theological institution in the country.
He bought the Carmelite property with the finest facilities
from the Roman Catholic Church and donated it to the
school. His wealth, his ideas, and his leadership made a
dream come true. But as always he was mindful of the ad-
monition in the Gospel of Matthew: "Take heed that you do
not your alms before men, to be seen of them: Otherwise,
ye have no reward of your Father which is in Heaven. Therefore, when thou doest thine alms, do not sound a trumpet before thee, as the hypocrites do in the synagogues and in the
streets, that they may have glory of men. Verily, I say unto
you, they have their reward. But when thou doest alms, let
not thy left hand know what thy right hand doeth." (Matthew
6: 1-3)

Mr. Pew mostly worked through the Pew Memorial Foundation which the Pew brothers and sisters had organized in 1948 in honor of their father. The original gift of 800,000 shares of Sun Oil Company grew with stock dividends, stock splits and more gifts to more than 6 million shares at the time of his death. It made grants to nearly all religious, charitable, and educational facets of our lives. It supported the United Fund, the Boy Scouts, the Girl Scouts, the YMCA's, many independent colleges, especially Negro colleges, such as Hampton and Bishop, the United Negro College Fund, numerous hospitals especially in the Philadelphia area, medical research, the Cancer Fund, the Billy Graham Crusades, the better seminaries across the country, some Bible Colleges, Youth for Christ, Young Life, *Christian Economics, Christianity Today, Presbyterian Layman,* The Foundation for Economic Education, and many others.

J. Howard Pew's most enduring object of philanthropy probably was his Alma Mater, Grove City College. His father had guided the school as Chairman of the Board ever since its reorganization in 1895. As if forewarned of his early death, Joseph Newton, in 1912, recommended that his son, J. Howard, and his nephew, John G., be elected to the Board so that "they should have outside tasks and interests." Throughout his long life J. Howard served the College with singular dedication. He was elected Chairman of the Board in 1931, a position he held until his death in 1971.

Under his guidance the College grew to one of the finest institutions of higher learning. In an industry that generally thrives on government largess, he built what is probably the most efficient educational organization whose operating costs and, consequently, tuition to its students, are the lowest of any private institution anywhere. At student cost not much higher than that of state colleges and universities with their subsidies of millions of tax dollars, over 2000 Grove City College students currently are receiving an excellent education. Through managerial efficiency, he endeavored to make higher education accessible to every able student, no matter how rich or poor his parents happen to be.

Mr. Pew had the vision of creating an entirely new campus, the "upper campus" on a hillside adjoining the old site in the heart of Grove City. With the help of prominent Boston architects, the Olmstead Brothers Company, who had designed New York's Central Park, the College slowly built an exceptionally beautiful campus. In such a setting many thousands of students hopefully acquired a vivid sense of the beautiful and the morally good, and above all, an understanding of Christian values.

J. Howard Pew's great interest in economic education led him, in 1950, to join the Board of Trustees of the Foundation for Economic Education in Irvington-on-Hudson, New York. Leonard Read, its founder and president, was struggling to make FEE a stronghold of moral values and economic ideas that sustain a free society. On the Board, J. Howard Pew found a remnant of kindred souls, successful industrialists and eminent scholars, who shared with him a great concern about the future of individual freedom and the private property order. Here, among his philosophical and ideological peers he would relax and enjoy the lively debates on the burning problems of our time. But above all, he would gain new hope and confidence in the rebirth of liberty and Western civilization.

J. Howard Pew aspired to neither wealth nor fame. And yet, his deeds brought forth their harvest in both great wealth and public recognition. In his lifetime he received, among others, American Petroleum Institute's Gold Medal for Distinguished Achievement, 1949; the Vermilye Medal of the Franklin Institute of Philadelphia, for achievements in management, 1950; the Pennsylvania Society's Gold Medal for distinguished achievement in humanitarian and civic fields, 1958; the Greater Philadelphia Chamber of Commerce's William Penn Award "for his monumental contribution to the well-being of the Delaware Valley Region," 1970; and the Magna Charta Award of the Baronial Order of Magna Charta for "his service to humanity" and for "his championing of freedom of the individual," 1971.

On November 27, 1971 J. Howard Pew departed this life. At his funeral the Reverend Billy Graham expressed the prayer of many:

We thank Thee and praise Thee for all that he meant to so many people for so long.

Two

●

Obedience to the Will of God

"If we would have faith in the Biblical sense, we must first accept Christ as Our Lord and Saviour and then, through the power of the Holy Spirit, make our will subject to God's will."[*]

To J. HOWARD PEW religion was not only a dogma, but also a service. The true divine of his religion was a life that is begotten of grace and that surrenders to God all the powers of heart and mind. It was a life of steady service—doing the will of God. In many of his speeches Pew stressed this aspect of his religion. "One of the greatest sermons I ever heard," he told the Presbyterian Men's Council on March 3, 1965, "was delivered by no less a dignitary than Prime Minister Manning of the Province of Alberta, Canada. In that sermon he urged us to become involved in the things that hinder spiritual recovery; that no such recovery is possible unless the Bible is accepted as the infallible Word of God and unless sin and evil are condemned. It has well been said that silence gives consent, and that all that is necessary for evil to prevail is for good men to do nothing. Genuine spiritual recovery is possible only when Christian people become personally involved with Jesus Christ, in His death, personally involved with Him, in His resurrection, personally involved with Him as a living member of His body—the Church of which He Himself is the Head."

[*]J. Howard Pew Speech at Brigham Young University, February 11, 1969.

The real distinction between church members of this generation and those of the past, Pew believed, is their degree of involvement in the affairs of the world. While we are often reluctant to accept Christ as an all-sufficient Saviour, our forebears were not ashamed of the gospel of Christ. Their's was St. Paul's rallying cry to the early Christians, which was responsible for the phenomenal growth of the early church: "I am not ashamed of the Gospel of Christ, because it is the power of God unto salvation." It was also Howard Pew's light of true religion. He was an ardent believer in the Presbyterian Church doctrine and organization. And as a lifelong student of church history he was familiar with the important events in the history of Presbyterianism. To him this history was a voice forever sounding through the centuries the principles of virtuous conduct and revelation of Providence. God revealed himself in the facts of Church history as truly as in the creation of the world.

Devout Presbyterians like J. Howard Pew find their guiding lights in the church apostolic times and in the Swiss Reformation. While many of their churches in other countries are known by the original name "Reformed Church," the churches of British origin use some form of the name Presbyterian. They did not adopt the Reformation as a finished system of faith and order, but rather sought to reform the life of the church in the light of its local situation and its understanding of past failures. What bound these churches into a loose association were certain convictions of creed, form of church government, and the conduct of a Christian life. John Calvin for whom they are frequently named was their greatest spokesman.

English Presbyterianism reached its zenith of influence shortly before and during the Civil War (1642-1648), when the Pews left England and settled in Virginia. Contending with Episcopalians, Puritans and Independents (later Congregationalists) for supremacy, the Presbyterian-Parliamentary Party gained control of Parliament in 1640. It summoned an Assembly of Divines to advise it in religious matters and draft a completely new religious constitution for the Kingdom.

The assembly consisted of two ministers from each county of England, in addition to ten peers and twenty commoners. Holding their meetings in Westminster Abbey, they elaborated, after years of debate (1643-1649), a Confession of Faith, a Larger and Shorter Catechism, a Form of Government, and a Directory of Public Worship. To J. Howard Pew these documents ranked among the great works of the Reformation. Again and again he talked admiringly about the Westminster Divines as "the wisest Biblical scholars ever assembled under one roof." So ably did these men perform their task, that it has stood the test of time. After some 300 years, the Confession of Faith and the Larger and Shorter Catechism stand substantially unchanged.

One of the significant results of these conferences, according to Pew, was the voting of the 30 Parliamentarians. They had been appointed primarily for the purpose of safeguarding the influence of government over the Church. Nevertheless, when the vote was finally taken, all members of Parliament actually approved the principle that Christ is the Head of the Church and that He has appointed its governing body. Samuel Bolton, an outstanding member of this group, eloquently expressed the convictions of both lay and clergy:

> The Word of God and God in His Word; the Scripture and God in Scripture—is the only supreme, infallible and authoritative rule and judge of matters of doctrine and worship, of things to be believed and things to be done.

But the most significant outcome of the assembly, according to Pew, was yet another. In their great wisdom the Westminster Divines limited the Church to ecclesiastical affairs. They did so in no uncertain terms: "Synods and councils shall handle or conclude nothing but that which is ecclesiastical."

This stricture was to guide J. Howard Pew through some of the most strenuous religious encounters of his life.

The constitutional documents of the Westminster Assembly made a lasting impression on J. Howard Pew. But in the hands of 17th century Englishmen they met an odd fate. It is true the Scottish Church and the Scottish Parliament accepted them promptly, but the English Parliament chose to ignore the Assembly which, after all, was merely an advisory committee. And the English Church never even considered the Presbyterian ideals because of the growing power of the Independents. By the end of the 18th century Presbyterianism was alive in Scotland, but virtually extinct in England.

In the American colonies Scotch-Irish, English and other immigrants formed Presbyterian churches that were independent of any parent body in Great Britain. Although they frequently squabbled among themselves about church character and constitution, they were united in their opposition to the settling of Anglican bishops on the colonies. They took a vigorous part in the struggles leading to the American Revolution, which to them was a "Christian cause."

The most prominent Presbyterian figure of the American Revolution, according to J. Howard Pew, was John Witherspoon (1723-1794). By sermon, satire, debate, pamphlet and essay he distinguished himself as clergyman, educator and statesman. As president of the College of New Jersey (now Princeton University) he had the vision of its potentialities as a cultural center and the great ability to breathe life into the struggling little college. Although born and educated in Scotland, he was an enthusiastic American from his arrival. He was the only clergyman to sign the Declaration of Independence and played a laudable part in the Continental Congress both in debate and on committees. He especially distinguished himself for the soundness of his financial and monetary views that were later published in his *Essay on Money* (1786).

When, in 1787, John Witherspoon and many Presbyterian delegates convened in Philadelphia to write a Constitution for the Presbyterian Church they adopted the Confession of Faith and the Larger and Shorter Catechism substantially as written by the Westminster Divines. They, too, were convinced that the Bible was the inspired and infallible Word of God. They were not ashamed of the Gospel of Christ, and by their lives and witnesses they endeavored to spread it.

J. Howard Pew accepted the Bible as the infallible Word of God. The Apostles' Creed precisely defined his position— that is, he believed in historic, orthodox Christianity and the Constitution of his Church. To him God revealed himself in the facts of Christian history and heritage which he set out to defend. As President of the Board of Trustees of the General Assembly of the Presbyterian Church of the U.S.A. (later the Foundation of the Presbyterian Church), which he served from 1940 until his death, he proclaimed his witness untiringly. At a meeting on February 15, 1958, in New York, he testified thus:

"While the Foundation is primarily concerned with the acquisition and custody of funds, it is also dedicated to the preservation of a spiritual heritage of precept and principle which has come down to us almost unchanged, during the last 170 years. The heritage of which I speak is embodied in the Constitution of the Presbyterian Church in the United States of America.

"This great statement of church laws and beliefs was drawn up by the Synod of New York and Philadelphia, which began its deliberations on May 17, 1787, and completed its work in the following year. It is a cornerstone of Christian liberty, and the manner in which it was drawn up closely parallels that of another great charter of liberty—the Constitution of the United States which, by a striking historical coincidence, was being debated by the Constitutional Convention only a few blocks away at the same time.

"Indeed, many of the same ideals inspired both the members of the synod and the founders of our country, and we should not overlook the circumstance that it was Dr. John Witherspoon, a signer of the Declaration of Independence, who played one of the leading roles in drafting the Constitution of the Presbyterian Church, and subsequently presided over the first meeting of the General Assembly.

"Nor should we forget that just as Thomas Jefferson had written that 'all men . . . are endowed by their Creator with certain inalienable rights,' so the fathers of our Church, in a statement of preliminary principles to the Form of Government, wrote that 'they consider the rights of private judgment, in all matters that respect religion, as universal and inalienable.'

"Thus it was that freedom of the individual to exercise his private judgment in matters of conscience, became fundamental in the government of the Presbyterian Church in America, and has so continued for many generations.

"Today the issue is freedom, just as it was 170 years ago. Freedom under God has made America great—freedom of the conscience, which is man's right to exercise his private judgment—freedom of religion—freedom to dream, to think, to experiment, to invent, to match wits in friendly competition—freedom to be an individual. That is America's Christian heritage. That is America's strength.

"Christian people everywhere are seeking to eliminate poverty and illiteracy, and to care for those who are unable to look after themselves. Seeing such ills and much injustice, the Christian is tempted to invoke the police power of government to correct them. But Christ proclaimed the gospel of love, not of force. Police power produces resentment and ill will, stifles energy and destroys production. It never makes men kind and charitable. Only the love of Christ can do that.

"Changing human hearts is a slower process than changing laws, but it is far more certain to accomplish the desired results. Let the Church not appeal from God to Caesar, but let it devote its energy to that of promoting Christian grace— honesty, truth, fairness, generosity, justice and charity—in the hearts of men. Free Christian men will apply the gospel to all areas of life, to all human activities, to the individual in his life and work, and to society in all of its relationships. The Gospel of Jesus Christ is universal, all-embracing, and sufficient to meet the needs of all mankind."

J. Howard Pew believed in the Presbyterian Church and its basic doctrines and principles. To him it was a missionary church, converting, advancing, encompassing the world. It was an organization truly potent for uplifting society, yesterday, today and tomorrow. But unfortunately, there are those members who would like the Church to leave the ecclesiastical field and deal with all kinds of economic, social, and political matters. They are creating dissent and conflict within the Church and causing many good members to withdraw their support from the Church. Surely such a reaction will cure the situation by destroying the Church itself. They act like the man who had his arm amputated because he had a sore finger.

A free society, J. Howard Pew believed, is built on individual honesty, truth, fairness, generosity, justice and charity, all of which are attributes of Christianity. And as the Church is God's instrumentality for the world-wide dissemination of Christianity we must support the Church. If we believe it to err in some matters, let us strive to correct the error by working within the Church. As a good wife stays loyal to her husband although she may disagree with him occasionally, so should Christians stay loyal to their Church.

The Church is God's instrumentality to carry the Gospel to man. All its parts must pull together—its Clergy, its members and the corporate Church, which is management. All must speak with one voice that God alone is the Lord of Creation and that the only way to eradicate sin is by the redemptive power of the Gospel of Jesus Christ.

Howard Pew liked to illustrate the work of the Church by relating the story of the husband and wife who had an ugly quarrel. After they were finally exhausted they went out and sat down on the porch—he on one end and she on the other. For a time nothing was said; and then a magnificent team of horses pulling a wagon loaded with stone came slowly up the hill. As the team passed in front of the porch, the wife turned to her husband and said, "John, wouldn't it be wonderful if we could pull together like that?" John looked at the team for a moment and then replied, "Well, Mary, we could pull together just like that if we had only one tongue between us."

The genius of the Presbyterian system, according to Pew, is the vital role of the layman in the management of church affairs, conforming with the Biblical statement of the priesthood of all believers. In Edgar Guest's words which Mr. Pew liked to quote:

> When you see a church that's empty, though its doors are
>   open wide,
> It is not the church that's dying, it's the laymen that have died;
> For it's not by song or sermon that the Church's work is done;
> It's the laymen of the country who for God must carry on.

J. Howard Pew carried on with all his strength and force that came from his faith. He who believes is strong, and strong convictions lead to great deeds. In 1940, he assumed the Presidency of the Board of Trustees of the General Assembly of the Presbyterian Church, a position of great influence over his church. But the most important position any layman could hold was that of Chairman of the National Lay Committee of the National Council of the Churches of Christ in the United States of America, representing 34,000,000 Protestants. J. Howard Pew occupied this post from the beginning of the Committee in 1950 until its dissolution in 1955.

With his passion for truth and right, he upheld principles that last forever. Although he and his Committee often stood alone against the Protestant clergy, they defended the prin-

ciple that the Christian churches should not become involved
in economic or political controversy. And although they voted
alone, their vote was never lost. For Protestants the world
over, their's was an epoch-making stand. His final report to the
Committee is an important document in contemporary
church literature. It will be read and studied by clergy and
laypeople as long as the bitter struggle between secularism
and evangelism continues to divide the Christian churches.

"In the failure of this most important effort to bring about
an enduring partnership between the clergy and laity," J.
Howard Pew reports, "I feel a very real responsibility to provide a comprehensive and factual account of those steps
which led to the Board's action discontinuing lay participation.

"The members of the National Lay Committee gave lib-
erally of their time and energy in an effort to establish unity
in Protestant organization. Its members substituted for the
Board's Committee on Business and Finance until that Committee could be organized late in 1951, and even after that
continued to lend a helping hand. It supplied members to a
long list of the Council's assemblies, boards and committees.
It held yearly meetings of its members, and I shall long remember them for their high degree of spiritual inspiration.

"Throughout our Committee's term of life, it repeatedly
brought to the Council's attention the seriousness of the problems involved in its issuance of controversial statements and
studies in the fields of sociology, economics and politics;
and the danger inherent in speaking to official Washington
and the United Nations General Assembly in behalf of Protestantism on matters outside their field and for which they
possessed no mandate.

"We had been told at the Lay Committee's Princeton meeting, April 5-6, 1952, that laity had been absent in large degree
from the councils of organized Protestantism for decades.
The reappearance of independent and responsible laity in

the councils of the church was said by Dr. John A. Mackay at that meeting to be 'the most creative movement which had emerged in the recent history of the Christian Church.'

"However, as we participated in the discussions of the General Board, the Council's divisional assemblies and committees, we laypeople found ourselves not only deeply in the minority but often poles apart from the clergy who invariably outvoted us ten-to-one in these sessions. The whole membership of the Council was continuously aware of the inadequacy of lay participation in its deliberations. Many official reports emphasized this fact. For example, those of us present at the Council's General Assembly in Denver heard Bishop Oxnam, chairman of the Committee on Study and Adjustment report as follows:

> There has been a tendency in recent years to expect religious professionals to carry too heavy a share of those responsibilities which should be carried jointly by professionals and laity.

The members of the Lay Committee were often misunderstood in their urgency to keep the churches out of politics and their insistence on the primacy of evangelism. Our premise was that, instead of appealing to government, the church should devote its energies to the work of promoting the attributes of Christianity—truth, honesty, fairness, generosity, justice and charity—in the hearts and minds of men. We attempted to emphasize that Christ stressed not the expanded state but the dignity and responsibility of the individual.

"It was at a General Board meeting in Chicago, May 18-19, 1953, that we realized the extent and character of the philosophy held currently by most of the ordained executives and officers directing the work of the several denominational headquarters staffs, and therefore of the National Council. Their philosophy, it seemed to the Lay Committee, looked to an ever-expanding government. Clergy and laity active in organized Protestantism seemed to have lost the capacity to understand each other. We, as laypeople, were alarmed and unhappy as the National Council assumed the right to speak increasingly on subjects in which it was difficult to see ethical or spiritual content for that inarticulate and voiceless body called, '34,000,000 Protestants.'

"The Chicago Board meeting indicated beyond doubt that the time was not yet ripe for the partnership between clergy and laity we had envisioned with so much hope and enthusiasm when the National Council was organized, back in 1950.

"Laypeople, however, were not alone in questioning the Council's issuance of statements and studies in which ethical or spiritual content was absent or overshadowed by political implications. We learned that in the issuance of statements pastors of local churches were closer to laypeople and their thinking than were denominational executives and officers.

"How did it happen that the hopes and aspirations expressed by the Planning Committee and concurred in by the Chairman and the members of the Lay Committee failed so utterly of accomplishment? This much is certain—with few exceptions, the members of the Lay Committee had agreed to serve only because they had been assured that the new National Council would avoid the political involvements and controversies which had characterized the activities of the old Federal Council of Churches which was now superseded.

"I shall not discuss the steps by which the National Council was to follow substantially the policy of the Federal Council. These are enumerated in the report which follows this letter. It did, however, become increasingly evident with the passing of time that it was vital for the National Council to have functioning within its organization an autonomous lay group with the responsibility of interpreting the work of the Council to the laity, and of interpreting the viewpoint of the laity to the Council.

"On February 24, 1954, the Lay Committee's officers and Executive Committee addressed a letter to Bishop William C. Martin, then president of the National Council, and forwarded copies to the members of the Council's General Board. This letter in full is to be found in the appendix which follows the report. As you will note, this letter suggested that the Lay Committee must retain its planning and working entity; that the proposed integration of the Lay Committee members, one-by-one, into the more than seventy units of the Council was not the answer. The letter said further that members of the Lay Committee were presently participating in the work of a large number of the Council's divisions, boards and committees; and that further dissemination without being able to discuss problems and aspirations with an autonomous Lay Committee would cause the loss to the Council of these laypeoples' skills, experience and viewpoints. The letter emphasized that

> The overall view of the Council's work, plus the opportunity to review this composite picture, is essential to the keeping together of this group of 190 laypeople. If our primary task is to be the interpretation of the Council's work, then we must know the whole picture collectively, be organized to discuss it and plan its interpretation together.

The Executive Committee stressed that dissemination alone could only render us ineffectual, and mean the abandonment of the whole philosophy of a clergy-and-laity partnership.

"Our Committee's work seemed to the Executive Committee to be completed when we addressed our 'Lay Affirmation' to the Council's Committee on Policy and Strategy on September 13, 1954, and to the General Board on September 15, 1954, on the subject of 'Corporate Pronouncements of Denominational or Interdenominational Agencies.' While the

entire statement is to be found in the appendix, I quote here
one important paragraph:

> Our Committee believes that the National Council of the
> Churches impairs its ability to meet its prime responsibility
> when, sitting in judgment on current secular affairs, it be-
> comes involved in economic or political controversy having
> no moral or ethical content, promoting division where unity
> of purpose should obtain, nor do we believe that the National
> Council has a mandate to engage in such activities.

When the General Board took no action on this 'Lay Affirmation' beyond voting to receive the document with gratitude,
most of the members of the Lay Committee came finally to
the realization that a wide chasm existed between the thinking of the laity and the clergy and executives of the denominational bodies which comprise the National Council.

"One last effort was made to hold the support of the Lay
Committee without conferring upon its membership the opportunities or responsibilities which had been looked for
since the first discussion in July of 1950. This approach, however, did not come from the General Board but from the
Executive Committee of the Board of Managers of the General Department of United Church Men. The proposal was
reminiscent of the earlier unworkable situation that had
existed between 1950 and 1952 and called for constituting
the Lay Committee as a standing committee of United Church
Men but with even more limited autonomy, status and program than had heretofore been the lot of the Lay Committee.
Since the minimum conditions for continued existence as
fixed by the Executive Committee of the Lay Committee had
the support of the membership at large and were found to be
incompatible with the invitation tendered, the Chairman
found no alternative but to decline it, which he did in con-
currence with the prior approval of the Vice Chairman and
twenty-seven of the thirty-one members of the Executive Committee.

"Thus, on June 30, 1955, the Lay Committee ceased to exist as a Committee of the General Board. The partnership projected by the Planning Committee and subsequently thus described as a goal desired by the National Council officials, proved in practice to be one where lay men and women of the churches were expected to provide avenues of support for policies and programs largely determined by professionals.

"The members of the Lay Committee believed, and so stated, that the political adventures of the National Council in the fields of economic and political controversy would seriously hinder and not further Christian leadership in the pressing fields of evangelism, fellowship and education.

"It appears from the record that the National Council could find no room for opposition to the philosophies and practices carried over from the old Federal Council. Lacking the patience to resolve the basic problem, it has sought to bury it.

"But the issue still remains as one which must be resolved if the Protestant Christian witness of the great denominations which make up the membership of the National Council is to gain strength and not weakness from its activities.

"If our Christian witness is to flourish an effort must be made to develop stronger roots of leadership in the great and still largely untilled fields of Christian lay activity, both within and without denominational channels. This is the effort to which the members of the Lay Committee had hoped to add their strength. It is an effort which should be continued until a more resourceful lay leadership can effect that partnership between clergy and laity so vital to the welfare of Protestantism. The Lay Committee believes also that the Constitution of the National Council must be so amended as to permit real lay participation before it can speak authoritatively for the clergy and those who sit in the pews.

"The Chairman believes, as stated in the Affirmation of the Lay Committee, that the National Council's proper and legitimate field of activity transcends in importance all other areas of human activity and aspirations. He is convinced that until the problems crystallized by the experiences of the Lay Committee have been adequately dealt with the vitally necessary work of Christianity will not go forward with that unity of purpose between the clergy and laity essential for progress toward our common aim that God's Will be done on earth as it is in heaven.

"He trusts that efforts to discover a workable reconciliation of divergent views will be carried forward and that a program can be developed through which laity and clergy may more effectively work together for the greater glory of God and the redemption of all mankind."

But in spite of the laymen's fervent opposition to rising secularism and humanism, in 1965, the 177th General Assembly of the United Presbyterian Church set about rewriting the confessional position of the Church. The Westminster Confession was to be replaced by the "Confession of 1967" because many clergymen believed that the seventeenth century confessional document was inadequate to guide Presbyterians in the twentieth century. To J. Howard Pew this change of confessional standard was most disconcerting and alarming. To him this was another indication of the errors of doctrine and decline of faith that were creeping into all churches. They were dangerous errors, as a great deal of truth was mingled with them which affords them credibility and circulation. In a number of speeches he, therefore, opposed the 1967 Confession as a man-made document that is likely to lead astray. At a meeting called by the Pittsburgh Presbytery, on January 27, 1966, he made these critical remarks:

"The Confession of 1967 confronts the Presbyterian Church with a challenge concerning her faith in the Holy Scripture. It denies clearly the position held by Christendom for almost 20 centuries and affirmed by the Westminster Confession, that the Bible is the true Word of God.

"Is the Bible true or is it false? Is its claim to be the Word of God a fraud? Are the Scriptures a divine guide for faith and life, or is it a human and therefore an unreliable document? Has the Church received a new revelation of the Will of God, which supersedes the Bible?

"The 1967 Confession answers these questions in a way that gives deep concern to professing Christians. It claims to be an up-to-date document to challenge a new age. However, the new document is but, in many ways, a restatement of the criticisms of Scripture made by atheists and humanists down through the corridors of time.

"The framers of the new Confession state that the entire Westminster Confession depends on 'The Westminster teaching about the Bible itself.' It would therefore appear that the justification for the new Confession is that the Scripture is not the true Word of God. If they are successful in toppling the First Chapter of the Westminster Confession, then all subsequent chapters will be overthrown because their very foundation will have been removed.

"Another amazing fact is that the new Confession claims to be a clear and readable document for the average layman. Laymen who have read it, confess to confusion and bewilderment. The document is filled with ambiguous and undefined statements.

"The proof, of course, is in the reading. Let me compare seven contrasting statements in the two Confessions.

"1. The Confession of 1967 declares that the Christian religion possesses a human character, shaped by the cultural forms of its environment. The Westminster Confession asserts that the authority of the Holy Scriptures dependeth, not upon the testimony of any man or church, but wholly upon God.

"2. The Confession of 1967 deplores the Westminster declaration that the 66 books of the Bible are to be equated with the Word of God. The Westminster Confession equates the 66 books with the Word of God and declares that they have been inspired by God to be *the* rule of faith and life, and by His providential care kept pure in all ages.

"3. The Confession of 1967 blurs the distinction between heathen religions and the Christian religion and finds many parallels between them. The Westminster Confession maintains that other books, claiming to be revelations of God, are mere human writings and have no authority in the Church of God.

"4. The Confession of 1967 claims that the words of Scripture are the words of men; that they reflect current views of life; and that there are a variety of such views. The Westminster Confession affirms the Bible to be the very Word of God and that the persuasion of its infallible truth is from the inward work of the Holy Spirit.

"5. The Confession of 1967 does not consider the Bible to be a complete revelation of the Will of God; that forms of worship and church government may change. The Westminster Confession regards the Holy Scriptures as a *complete* rule of faith and life wherein the principles of worship and church government are clearly taught.

"6. The Confession of 1967 declares that to understand the Scriptures requires literary and historical scholarship. The Westminster Confession asserts that the unscholarly as well as the scholarly may attain to a sufficient understanding of Scripture by Faith.

"7. The Confession of 1967 declares that the Church must be guided by the Holy Spirit but makes no reference to Scripture. The Westminster Confession maintains that the only authoritative voice in the Church is the Holy Spirit speaking in the Scripture.

"It would appear that the committee who wrote the new Confession believes that the Scriptures mean one thing to one generation, and something quite different to another generation. It would also appear that as the environment in the east is quite different from that which obtains in the west, the

Christian religion taught should vary accordingly. It would also appear that this committee does not believe in such a thing as an eternal verity; and yet Christ said: 'Heaven and earth shall pass away but my Words shall not pass away.'

"The entire Confession of 1967 is built around the word 'reconciliation.' This word occurs 23 times in the 1967 Confession and not at all in the Westminster Confession. In fact, it occurs only 13 times in the entire Bible. But even in the 1967 Confession it is robbed of its basic Scriptural meaning.

"Reconciliation, as used in the Bible, means to restore to favor or friendship those who are at variance. It is used particularly in reference to the atoning work of our Lord upon the cross. When reconciliation is mentioned in the Scriptures, it is expressed by God's reconciling us unto Himself, and not by His being reconciled to us. God is the offended party, and we by our sins are the offenders. It is we who need to be reconciled to Him, and not He unto us. The 1967 Confession uses the word, not in the primary sense the Bible used it, but in order to reconcile man to man, which is a secondary concept. The First Commandment states, thou shalt love the Lord thy God with all thy heart and soul and mind; and the Second Commandment, thou shalt love thy neighbor as thyself. Unless there is love of God, we will not have love for our neighbor. Man will love God only when he is reconciled to God through faith in Jesus Christ.

"The 1967 Confession does not ring true. The good old Biblical words which mean so much to professing Christians, such as, Sanctification, Justification, Providence, Holy Scripture, Repentance, Redemption, Judgment, Adoption, Trinity, Saving Faith, Atonement, Deity of Christ, Christian Liberty, and Conscience—are all conspicuous by their absence.

"It may well be that the Confession of 1967 is designed to discredit the true meaning of the Scriptures so that the Church may be taken out of its ecclesiastical field and involved in the whole gamut of human affairs. If this is not its

purpose, why does it state: 'A Church which denies responsibility in economic affairs, can offer no acceptable worship to
God.'? Why are these men so determined to commit our
Church to a course of action which will destroy its effective-
ness, make of it a secular institution, and force a large pro-
portion of its members out of the Church?

"In the Middle Ages, the Church exercised such rigid control over the lives and activities of the people that the State
became a servant of the Church; and the Church, drunk with
power, became one of the most corrupt institutions in the
world. The Reformation was a revolt against this and other
errors which had crept into the Catholic Church. Does our
Church covet political power? Are we going to incorporate
in our Church the very evils against which our forebears
fought in order that we might be free? God forbid."

J. Howard Pew deeply believed that the dissemination of
Christian principles transcends in importance all other areas
of human activity and aspiration. With his great influence
and wealth he sought to promote Christian living and education. Therefore, he opposed without reservation any church
doctrine or policy that in his judgment would detract from the
Christian calling. He was in the forefront of the long and bitter battle against encroaching statism in the churches, doing
everything in his power to enlighten and instruct his fellowmen. He helped all kinds of church publications and gave
countless speeches on church doctrine and policy. To him St.
Paul had sounded the warning: "If the trumpet give an uncertain sound, who shall prepare himself for battle."

One of the journals he helped to form was *Christianity
Today.* It was designed to be an intellectual journal on theological conservatism and to become an influential religious
journal in America today. He helped it financially, served on
the board of directors, and wrote a few articles for publication. And although the board frequently voted against his
viewpoint he continued to serve the journal faithfully for

more than fifteen years. But he frequently stated his convictions with complete candor and integrity. At one of the meetings on June 25, 1964, he again spoke of his fear that the great religious institutions were endangered by statism and secularism, institutions that were built at great sacrifice by our Protestant fathers. "We are at war today," he proclaimed, "the most serious and devastating war that has ever been waged, a war against the Scripture, against the faith of our fathers."

He was convinced that most Protestant denominations have lost their religious moorings. In many respects they are violating their constitutions, codes, creeds or historical precedents. In the Presbyterian Church, the hierarchy is surreptitiously searching for ways and means to change the Church Constitution, not by rewriting it, but by making additions that directly conflict with other provisions of the Constitution. Then, in later years, they will point out the contradictions and remove the older portions.

There are those individuals who hold strong beliefs, and therefore tolerate nothing else. And there are others who tolerate everything because they believe in nothing. J. Howard Pew, with his dauntless faith in the teachings of Christ and the Apostles, would not tolerate surrender of Christian institutions to Caesar, nor would he suffer the Church to meddle in the affairs of Caesar. Even if the Church were to possess competence and knowledge in political affairs, which it surely does not, it still should abstain from any involvement for reasons of jurisdiction. The Church can speak authoritatively on ecclesiastical matters only.

And yet, J. Howard Pew was most tolerant toward all other churches that seek to reach the hearts and minds of men, rather than the seats of political power. He thought highly of the Church of Jesus Christ of Latter-Day Saints and its institutions of higher learning. In a speech to more than 11,000 Brigham Young University students, on February

11, 1969, he lauded the University and its great President, Ernest L. Wilkinson, for raising the most loyal and law-abiding citizens in this country. And he reminded them that at the time of Christ the economic and social conditions were far worse than today. There was great corruption in government; immorality, intolerance, extortion and cruelty were everywhere. Christ knew all about these things, but he never planned a protest march or instigated a riot. He held himself aloof from all civil affairs and did not interfere with the administration.

While Mr. Pew strenuously opposed the secular and humanist tendencies of his own church hierarchy, he enjoyed the respect and trust of many church leaders outside the Presbyterian Church. Several bishops of the Roman Catholic Church, and especially the archbishop of Philadelphia, shared his great concern about the rise of statism and therefore esteemed his courageous stand. A strong and enduring bond of understanding and sympathy united them.

A positive character, with a positive faith, positive opinions and positive actions not only creates many enemies but also attracts the friendship of other positive men. The most influential American clergyman during the 1960's and 1970's, Billy Graham, considered J. Howard Pew one of his closest friends, advisors and confidants. "I came to respect his advice and his counsel," Reverend Graham disclosed. "I have gone to him on so many occasions for advice and counsel in my work, I came to love him as almost a father. When I think of J. Howard Pew I think of total integrity. You may not agree with his views, but you have to admit that he is a man of complete integrity. He need not sign anything—his word is his bond. I think his generation had a strength of character that is missing today."

On several occasions Mr. Pew was nominated for the position of elder in his church. He finally accepted, at the age of 76, after thorough preparation and serious meditation. He carefully read John Calvin's *Institutes of the Christian Religion*, the superb normative statement of reformed theology. Calvin himself had conceived this work as a guide to Bible study, and therefore organized it into four books in the sequence of doctrines in the ancient Apostles' Creed—Creator, Redeemer, Spirit and Church. Thus prepared, J. Howard Pew was elected and ordained ruling elder for the government and the discipline of his congregation on January 26, 1958.

One of the last speeches he was to give, on September 15, 1970, was to the Women's Association of his own congregation, the Ardmore Presbyterian Church. Under the title "The Church Today" he summarized his great concern about the future of church and country.

"Of all the institutions in the world, the Christian Church is surely the most amazing. Standing like a rock amid the shifting currents and cultures of the ages, it has occupied a unique place in the minds and hearts of men for almost 2,000 years. While other institutions have come and gone, economic and political systems waxed and waned, the Church alone among them all had endured. And this is surely a miracle.

"The history of Presbyterianism is a romantic story in which men of great Biblical scholarship and dedication have guided it wisely and well down through the centuries. I believe in the Presbyterian Church and in the concepts upon which it has been builded. I believe that it is one of the great uplifting forces in our society; that it will survive not only this generation but many generations to come. I believe that as the years roll on its influence for good will ever increase and that it will ever contribute to the greater glory of God and the redemption of mankind.

"But unfortunately, our denomination is temporarily being unduly influenced by a small group of church leaders who are determined to change our Church from a religious institution to a secular one. Many of these church leaders believe that the Revelations of the Prophets are the words of men and not the words of God. There are some 3,600 places in the Bible where the words 'God saith' or their equivalent are used to support the Revelations of the Prophets as the words of God. Many of these church leaders do not believe in the supernatural. Now, the Resurrection, the Atonement, the Virgin Birth, miracles, the efficacy of prayer, and the Divinity of Christ are all supernatural. It is difficult for me to understand how anyone can think of himself as a Christian who denies these fundamental Christian concepts. Many of these church leaders believe that the true mission of the Church is to reconcile man to man, whereas the Bible tells us that God reconciled man unto Himself. Many of these church leaders are humanists, and humanism, according to their own manifesto, has almost the same objectives as has communism. If there be any difference, it is that humanism is a little the worse. Many of these church leaders believe, as does Dr. Niles, one of the leaders of the World Council of Churches, that the heart of Christianity is not concern for the soul, but concern for the world. In order to effectuate their objectives, many of these church leaders are now openly advocating revolution.

"Materialism, secularism, humanism, socialism, and Marxism have all infiltrated most of our Protestant denominations. As Dr. Billy Graham so aptly put it: 'Christ said in His Sermon on the Mount, *Beware of false prophets which come to you in sheep's clothing, but inwardly they are ravening wolves.* Then He significantly added, *By their fruits ye shall know them.*' Many of our Protestant denominations are losing their influence by listening to these false prophets.

"As a result of the influence of these humanists, many of our larger denominations have issued statements and pronouncements urging our government to recognize Red China and Communist Cuba; to close our Latin American bases; to abandon the ABM system; to bring our troops home from Viet Nam; to boycott South Africa; to cease all nuclear developments; and to in many other ways promote the interests of Communism.

"Presbyterianism has always upheld the right of dissent. This is a most important right, provided, of course, it is applied in a way which is honest, fair, equitable, and just. My great concern, however, is that many of our church leaders hold that it is perfectly proper for the humanists to exercise their right of dissent by refusing to obey our laws, whereas when I dissent, it becomes divisive.

"If, in our larger denominations, conservative, evangelical, Bible-believing Christians, who prefer the theology of reformation to the theology of revolution, cannot enunciate their beliefs without having their motives questioned and their character maligned; if one cannot express his honest differences of opinion without subjecting himself to the charges of disunion and divisiveness; if non-Christian liberals who would overthrow the government and destroy our capitalistic system are hailed by our church leaders as prophets of our time; if those who have supported the doctrine on which our churches were founded are accused of upsetting the peace, unity, and purity of the Church—then, indeed, our churches are in deep trouble.

"Now that our church has moved out of its ecclesiastical field, it would be interesting to know why it was silent when the Russians invaded Czechoslovakia, or when the communists committed mass murder in Viet Nam, or, more importantly, when literally millions upon millions of Chinese were murdered when the communists took over the country there. And why is it that even the mention of communism evokes angry charges of McCarthyism, Fascism, and the like? And now that I am on the subject, why is it that pornography and immorality and other unChristian activities are not denounced by our churches; and why do they not commend the attributes of Christianity—honesty, truth, fairness, generosity, justice, and charity?

"There never was a time when it was more important to discuss our differences in Christian love than it is today. I have always greatly admired the Westminster Divines, primarily because they were seekers of truth. As you will recall, they were assigned the task of determining what constituted the true Church based on the Bible. At the outset, there was a vast difference of opinion among them, but after years of prayerful discussion they unanimously approved the Westminster Confession of Faith, save for one vote.

"Let me tell you a story. An old farmer came home one night after a hard day's work and found his wife desperately ill. The doctor was sent for post-haste. He arrived shortly and spent some time with the patient. As he emerged from the sickroom, he was accosted by the old farmer. 'Doctor,' asked the farmer, 'Did you find out what was wrong with her?' 'No,' replied the doctor, 'I was unable to diagnose her case.' 'Oh,' moaned the old farmer, 'Is there no hope?' 'Oh yes,' replied the doctor, 'She is going to get well. I have given her some medicine that will throw her into fits, and you know I'm a great expert on fits.'

"And so it is with these humanists. They believe there is something wrong with our economic system, something wrong with our educational system, something wrong with our medical system; in fact, they think there is something wrong with all of our ways of life. They don't know what it is that is wrong, but they do know that whatever it is, a good dose of humanistic communism will cure it.

"Most people today believe that because we have made such great progress in technology and atomic energy, that similar progress has been made in all other human activities. But this is simply not true. There are a great many areas in which we have suffered a severe deterioration. For example, in England we find the greatest Biblical scholars of all time back in the 17th century. We should not be confused by the sophistry of these ultra-liberal church leaders but should adhere to the sound doctrine laid down by our church fathers.

"Jesus was sent into this world in order that it might be made a better and a finer place in which to live and to work. He knew that this objective could not be accomplished by any human or earthly means; that it could be achieved only by the regeneration of men's hearts through the power of the Holy Spirit. The people sought to induce Christ to accept an earthly throne, but His answer was: 'My Kingdom is not of this world.'

"Protestantism has always taken the position that the Christian, as an individual, has the responsibility to become involved in all such economic, social, and political affairs for which he possesses knowledge and competence. However, when an individual church or a church council composed largely of clergymen issues statements on complex economic, social, and political affairs, leaving the public with the impression that they are speaking for their entire membership, the result is justifiable indignation on the part of the laity. 'When I joined the Church,' writes a layman from Oak Ridge, Illinois, 'I stated my faith in Jesus Christ as my personal saviour. I wasn't asked to subscribe to any economic, social, or political issue. Is this now about to be changed?' he asked. Christ made his position crystal clear on this point when He said: 'Render unto Caesar the things that are Caesar's, and unto God the things that are God's.' John Calvin, the father of the Reformed tradition, was one of many who flatly stated that the Church has no Scriptural authority outside of the ecclesiastical field.

"Most of our seminaries have fallen into the control of these so-called humanists and no longer teach the Bible as the inspired, infallible, and authoritative Word of God, but rather as a historic document in which the writer is witness to the events of the time. Students are taught to be relevant to the time; to engage in social action; to fight for the material rights of the underprivileged; to resist laws they believe unjust; and to become knowledgeable in economics, politics, government, anthropology, psychology, sociology, situation ethics, and so on. The result has been that these seminaries are now turning out untrained social workers who have very little knowledge of the Bible, Christian teaching, or sound theology. Small wonder that so many of them break down. The records indicate that there are more suicides and mental breakdowns among the young ministers than are to be found in any other professional group.

"Our Presbyterian denomination was established to give laymen a voice in the ruling affairs of the church. Our church government was set up to be governed by ruling elders. Ministers were ordained as teaching elders. But it has not worked out that way. In too many instances the ruling elders have abdicated their responsibilities and by default the government of the Church has fallen onto the shoulders of the ministers. Thus, a minister must devote more and more of his time to administrative affairs, committee meetings, and the like, leaving less and less of his time to the teaching and preaching of the Gospel.

"The Presbyterian Lay Committee believe that the vast majority of the laity know the Bible to be the inspired, infallible, and authoritative Word of God, and that they are hungry to hear the Word of God preached and the truths of the Bible defended in their pulpits. Too often, however, they do not realize that many of our church leaders have departed far from the faith of our fathers. The time has now come when we must put our Church back in its proper perspective—time that we take our lay responsibilities seriously. This is the reason that the Presbyterian Lay Committee has devoted so much of their time and energy to getting the Church back to its proper mission—that of saving souls.

"The Church is the great hope, if not the only hope, of the

world. If it proclaims the Bread of Life as it did in the past, it will so affect society that it will eliminate most of its ills. But if it continues to cast doubts on the power of God to redeem society by transforming human nature, it will make the same ideological mistake as was made by communism: that of attempting to change society by changing man's environment.

"Saint Paul did not hesitate to become involved when he wrote that ringing statement to the Church at Rome—'I am not ashamed of the Gospel of Christ, for it is the power of God unto salvation to everyone that believeth.'

"When Saint Paul said 'I am not ashamed of the Gospel of Christ' he meant far more than had he said: 'I am not ashamed of Christ.' For there are many who accept Christ who have many reservations about accepting His Gospel.

"Saint Paul was not ashamed of the Gospel because he was not ashamed of its Divine Founder, Our Lord and Saviour, Jesus Christ. He was not ashamed of the great miracle by which Christ came into the world, or the miracles which Christ eventually performed. Nor was he ashamed of the teachings and precepts of Christ, nor of Christ as a Christian friend.

"In the early days of the Christian Church, Pagan Rome did everything humanly possible to destroy the followers of Christ. Some were crucified; others were thrown to the lions; some were sewn up in the skins of wild beasts and torn to pieces by savage dogs; others were smeared with tar and burned as torches at night. Every known torture was employed to force the early Christians to recant. But their cry always was: 'I am not ashamed of the Gospel of Christ, for it is the power of God unto salvation.' This greatest of all Biblical texts provided these early Christians with the courage to resist Pagan Rome. These early Christians were so proud to become involved with Christ they were willing to make any sacrifice, even unto death.

"In the 10th and 11th centuries, we read of a people who were not ashamed of the Gospel of Christ. They were known as the Waldensians. These Waldensians lived in villages hidden away in the inaccessible valleys of the Alps. Theirs was a precarious existence. Crops were uncertain and periodically their religious enemies sent their armies in to burn their villages and massacre the people. But they were undaunted. The Bible was their buttress and their shield. They were the first evangelists as we know them today.

"Waldensian preachers, disguised as itinerant merchants, traveled far and wide. They dealt in silks and precious stones. They sought entrance to the homes of the nobility, where, after disposing of their wares and then being asked if they had anything else to sell, would reply: 'Yes, we have something far more precious than anything which you have seen. If you will not tell the clergy we will show you a gem which shines so brightly that it will kindle the love of God in the heart of its possessor.' Then they would tenderly unwrap the package and disclose the Bible.

"Whittier, in one of his famous poems, tells the story of such a preacher in these words:

> O lady fair, I have yet a gem
>   Which a purer luster flings
> Than the diamond flash of the jewelled crown
>   On the lofty brow of kings.
> A wonderful pearl of exceeding price
>   Whose virtue shall not decay;
> Whose light shall be as a spell to thee
>   And a blessing on thy way!

And then the lady, being intrigued with the opportunity of acquiring a precious gem, offered to pay his price in gold, and these lines follow:

> The Cloud went off from the pilgrim's brow
>   As a small and meager book
> Unchased with gold or diamond gem.

> From his folding robe he took:
> 'Here, lady fair, is the pearl of price—
> May it prove as such to thee!
> Nay, keep thy gold—I ask it not—
> For the Word of God is free.'

These Waldensians were so proud to become involved with Christ that they, too, were willing to make any sacrifice.

"In the 16th Century came the Reformation. Many of these reformers were killed by their religious enemies. But they never hesitated to become involved. Had they not become involved, Protestantism today would be unknown.

"Then came the Westminster Divines and our own church fathers.

"Every one of these great church leaders believed that it was their Christian duty to become involved. There is a vast difference between the churchmen of today and those of the past. Today we do not want to become involved, whereas our forebears were not ashamed of the Gospel of Christ.

"I spoke a few moments ago about the humanists. These humanists represent a small minority in most of our larger denominations. They are a vociferous and militant group and do not hesitate to become involved. The result has been that this small minority, who are always willing to become involved, are exercising a far greater influence on the policies and objectives of our denominations than are the majority. The Presbyterian Lay Committee believe that unless the laymen in their denomination can be persuaded to become involved, there is no hope to save our denomination from becoming a secular institution.

"Are we willing to become involved? If we are not, we will lose our respect for ourselves, and our self-respect is our most precious asset. Many years ago Edgar Guest wrote a little poem, which expresses what I have in mind far better than any words of mine could. It runs something like this:

I have to live with myself and so
I want to be fit for myself to know.
I want to be able as days go by
Always to look myself straight in the eye.
I don't want to sit by the setting sun
And hate myself for the things I've done.

I don't want to keep on a closet shelf
A lot of secrets about myself,
And fool myself as I come and go
Into thinking that nobody else will know
The kind of a man I really am;
I don't want to live a life of sham.

I want to walk with my head erect,
And always keep my self-respect;
But here in the struggle for fame and pelf,
I want to be able to like myself,
I don't want to think as I come and go
That I'm bluster and bluff and empty show.

I never can hide myself from me;
I see what others may never see;
I know what others may never know;
I never can fool myself—and so,
Whatever happens, I want to be
Self-respecting and conscience free.

Three

●

America, the Home of Freedom
and Hope of the World

It is my conviction that it was freedom that effected the miracle of America—intellectual freedom, religious freedom, political freedom, industrial freedom; freedom to dream, to think, to experiment, to invent, to match wits in friendly competition; freedom to be an individual. That is our great American heritage.*

DURING THE EIGHTY-NINE YEARS of J. Howard Pew's life America ascended to become the most prosperous and powerful country in the world. Since 1882, Americans trebled the supplies of goods and services available per person and made great qualitative improvement in their living conditions. Better quality consumer's goods and services, such as food, clothing, housing, transportation, education, medical services, and countless other items are available today, frequently even at lower prices than in 1882. Their phenomenal economic progress affords more time for leisure, education, and other interests. In 1882, the average industrial work day was almost eleven hours. It fell to ten during the 1890's, to nine in 1914, to eight in 1940, and today to less than eight with a five-day week and several weeks of paid vacation. During that span of eighty-nine years, the U.S. population grew from 53 million to 208 million, and individual life expectancy rose from some 43 years to about 70. If human life is mankind's

*J. Howard Pew Speech before Philadelphia Council of Churches, June 3, 1952.

most cherished possession, the economic achievements of Americans have indeed been most bountiful and beneficent.

Throughout his long life J. Howard Pew was a fervent American, proud of his country's heritage and achievements. To him America was another name for opportunity and excellence, for elevation of the masses of humanity to decent living and self-respect. To him America held out a shining example to the human race. In a speech to the Teachers' Institute of Delaware County, Pennsylvania on October 30, 1944, in the midst of a devastating war, he described his image of America:

"Freedom for the individual and opportunity for individual initiative! These few words summarize America's history and point to the promise of hope for the future. An unquenchable thirst for freedom brought the founders of our country across the seas to this land. Here they created a system of freedom under which each had the opportunity to employ his talents as he desired so long as he did not injure his neighbor. Here the only class distinction was one earned through ability and hard work. Men and women were rewarded in accordance with that ability and industry. Never before have men and women had such opportunities nor have they ever had such incentives to drive them on to their achievement. The result was the building of the greatest nation on earth— a nation which has enjoyed the highest standard of living in all history—a standard of living which before this war was almost three times that of any other nation on earth.

"Today the world is trembling under the impact of a horrible war. We know we shall win that war because of the heroism of our fighting men and women and our great industrial capacity, converted to making weapons of war. In the days ahead of us our strongest anchors will be found in our American history—in the story of our institutions, in our traditions and in our truly American philosophy of individual freedom and personal opportunity for all. Thus to win the peace at home, our greatest weapon will be a thorough and an accurate understanding of American history."

In war and peace J. Howard Pew was mindful of the genius of America, mindful that freedom means more than personal security, or appeasement of tyranny as the price of peace. He liked to quote Kipling's "Dane-Geld" on that point:

It is always a temptation to an armed and agile nation
    To call upon a neighbour and to say:
"We invaded you last night—we are quite prepared to fight,
    Unless you pay us cash to go away."

It is always a temptation to a rich and lazy nation
    To puff and look important and to say:
"Though we know we should defeat you, we have not the time to meet you,
    We will therefore pay you cash to go away."

It is wrong to put temptation in the path of any nation,
    For fear they should succumb and go astray;
So when you are requested to pay up or be molested,
    You will find it better policy to say:

"We shall never yield to any threat,
    No matter how trifling the cost;
For the end of that game is oppression and shame,
    And the nation that plays it is lost!"

In World War II few Americans, if any, contributed more to the ultimate victory of American forces than J. Howard Pew. His foresight and initiative led his company to build 250 major vessels, to repair 1200 ships in its drydocks, to construct 40 per cent of all tankers built in the U.S. or more than the entire British Empire was able to build; to deliver oil and gasoline to all theaters of the war—Greenland, Iceland, Scotland, the Mediterranean, Russia, the Persian Gulf, Australia, and many Pacific islands—on Sun tankers traveling 2,358,000 miles carrying 41 million barrels of aviation gasoline and other petroleum products, and to produce the high octane gasoline that fueled more than half of all American Army and Navy planes in 1942 and 1943. The Houdry process which Sun Oil had developed before the war vitally contributed to this achievement. It was another example of J. Howard Pew's entrepreneurship. In the midst of the Great Depression, with gasoline a glut on the market following the discovery of the giant East Texas Field, Sun Oil risked millions of dollars on a process to make still more gasoline. What interested J. Howard was the quality of the gasoline it produced, as well as the yield per barrel, which had conservation implications—that is, ability to fuel more cars at a lower rate of crude oil consumption. Sun's development of the process to commercial-scale application, and licensing of the process to others at reasonable royalty costs, meant that some 14 Houdry Catalytic Cracking plants were operating in the U.S. when the battles raged in the skies of Europe and the Pacific.

World War II was primarily a contest in production. American industry and agriculture were called upon to outproduce the combined efforts of the enemy. The industrial executive, the mechanic, the refinery and shipyard workers, the farmer and all other producers were not just "the men behind the gun," but the vanguard of the forces of the free society. That's why they needed to be free to produce efficiently and economically, to develop new defense products and processes. No Federal government could be expected to win the war, it could only lose it by stifling man's productive energy.

To illustrate this point Mr. Pew liked to cite a few interesting examples of American military history. In a speech to the National Industrial Information Committee on June 30, 1941, he remarked:

"If there is one field in which invention should be in the van under Government auspices, one might assume that it would be in the field of the military industries. But what has been our experience in that regard? It has been, broadly, that Government producers of the mechanisms and munitions of war have had to rely mainly on civilian genius and inventive-

ness. I may cite a couple of illustrations from the history of
the firearm development. The first has to do with the Pennsylvania rifle. The British regulars in the Revolutionary War
were armed with the good old Brown Bess musket, a short-
barreled, smooth-bore weapon, so rudimentary that in the
hands of the best marksman it had a fair chance of hitting
something, but probably not the intended target. Somebody
said it was usually accurate enough to hit a barn, provided it
was shot off inside the barn. On the other hand, an American gunsmith at Lancaster, Pennsylvania, had discovered the
trick of rifling a gun barrel—cutting a spiral groove inside the
barrel, to give the bullet a rotary movement. Lengthening
and rifling his gun barrel, he produced a weapon unrivaled
for accuracy. When the Pennsylvania volunteers from the
backwoods counties joined Washington before Boston wearing coonskin caps, buckskin jackets and leather leggins, and
carrying these ridiculously long squirrel rifles, they were the
object of much derision—until it was discovered that they
could actually hit the things that they were shooting at and
over such long distances that the boys in red uniforms simply
didn't have a chance. At Bunker Hill it was alleged that the
Pennsylvania riflemen simply mowed them down. Washington, with plenty of frontier experience, knew all about the
Pennsylvania rifle, and he wanted to equip as many as possible of his troops with them. But the Continental Congress
was no better equipped with imagination than Governmental
agencies invariably have been: Washington got a very limited supply of these rifles. Nevertheless, the deadly marks-
manship of his Pennsylvanians so terrorized the British and
Hessian troops that Washington adopted a bit of strategy.
He uniformed companies of troops in the coonskin and
leather regalia of the Pennsylvanians, and the sight of them
was enough to start panic in the enemy's ranks. There is a
highly respectable body of military men who believe that the
Pennsylvania rifle, plus this uniforming ruse, was the deter-

mining factor in winning the Revolution. But the Government at Philadelphia never really did find out what the Pennsylvania rifle was doing for it.

"There is another story about Government ineptness that I think I must tell, by way of emphasis. A few years after our War of Independence, Europe was in the turbulence of the French Revolution, and, just exactly as today, our own peace was threatened. Just as today, also, Government tardily discovered that it was sadly unprepared to defend itself in a crisis. So it contracted with Eli Whitney, a Yankee machinist who was just coming into fame for his invention of the cotton gin, to make ten thousand muskets. Whitney had a firearms factory in Connecticut, and he started on his big contract in a way that shortly convinced the wiseacres that he was a bit crazy. He didn't start making muskets. Instead, he set about building a series of strange machines, none of which had any apparent relationship to the musket. A year passed, and he hadn't turned out a single gun. His contract required that the ten thousand muskets must be delivered within two years. Plainly enough, if he couldn't show one gun at the end of one year, he couldn't be expected to deliver his ten thousand guns at the end of the second year. Criticism and complaint reached his ears, but he calmly went ahead building his strange machines. One of them was made to bore out the barrels, another to form the stocks, and various others to make all kinds of parts. Then one day, when he was threatened with losing his contract for failure to perform, Whitney filled a bag with miscellaneous parts of a musket, and went to Washington. He dumped the bag on a long table and told his critics that there were the parts for ten muskets: they were invited to fit the parts together into ten complete weapons.

"Whitney had invented the process of using machinery to manufacture machinery; turned out from the precision operation of his machines, the parts were exactly alike, standardized and interchangeable. They could be made at almost incredible speed and very little highly skilled labor was required. Eli Whitney, in short, had invented the revolutionary process of mass production. He had done it in the face of the sharpest criticism and hostility in Governmental quarters. But seeing was believing. At least, the Government satrap didn't take his contracts away from him; and that perhaps was as much as Government could decently be expected to contribute to the greatest single advance ever achieved in industrial processes.

"I have recalled these illustrations of Governmental ineptitude for recognizing, understanding and dealing with the work of inventors, scientists and industrialists, with no purpose of criticizing Government and its administrators. In the very nature of things the Governmental process must be essentially conservative. The type of mind, in the inventor or the enterpriser, that dares to contemplate revolutionary change with entire equanimity, is exactly the type of mind most dangerous when trusted with the functions of Government. Government, in an enlightened society, must be the guardian of the accumulated achievements of civilization through the ages. I know in recent time we have seen many cynical disavowals of that responsibility. But those very disavowals, and the barbarities which have accompanied them, have only served to make decent people realize how sacred is the trusteeship that society places in the hands of its rulers. Such brutal excesses as the burning of the books, the closing of the universities, the outlawing of intellect and the degradation of culture are storm signals to us. They warn us how grave a danger is involved in the departure of Government from its function as conservator of whatever has been tried and approved in the long evolution of human institutions. The field of adventure and experiment should be left to the genius and initiative of free enterprise. Only by putting Government and enterprise each in its rightful place, shall we establish a proper balance in the social structure."

War, even in defense of public liberty, was a dreaded evil to J. Howard Pew. It gives rise to government debts and taxes, breeds discretionary powers of the executive and greatly extends its influence over the social and economic affairs of the people. It is the great destroyer of individual freedom and, when waged continually, even weakens the public will to be free.

In World War II the Federal government severely hampered the productive efforts of American industry by imposing a great many orders, measures and edicts. In an address to the Bond Club of Philadelphia on April 14, 1943, J. Howard Pew singled out a few that, in his judgment, were most destructive to industrial initiative and efficiency. For instance, he lamented the renegoiation of contracts. "What incentive is there for any organization to improve their efficiencies and reduce their costs," he asked, "when they know beforehand that every dollar so saved must eventually be paid over to the Government when their contracts are renegotiated?" Then, there was the $25,000 salary limitation which singled out for punishment "the very men who, more than any others, have been responsible for this magnificent record of war production." There was the drive to eliminate advertising as a "waste of manpower." In turn, this drive, in conjunction with a severe reduction in paper allocation, was destroying the press through depriving its members from earning a livelihood. And finally, Mr. Pew was alarmed about the government program to conscript and regiment industrial labor. "The initiative of the American workers," Pew pointed out, "has long been outstanding as compared with other countries. When they are deprived of their freedom to work where they please, they then become slave labor. Slave labor will produce but a fraction of what the workers are now turning out. I predict that in the event labor is conscripted in industry, production will never again achieve its present peak, irrespective of the number of additional men who may here-after be thrown into industry.

"This war can never be won in Washington but it can be lost there. When this war is over, it will have been won by the initiative of industry, business and agriculture, for this is a war of production. Those of us who are primarily responsible for production must learn to take the punitive measures coming out of Washington and in spite of them keep going strong. This requires a very special kind of philosophy. A short time ago I found this philosophy depicted in this little poem:

GOIN' STRONG!

His hoss went dead an' his mule went lame,
He lost six cows in a poker game;
An' a hurricane come on a summer's day,
An' carried the house whar he lived away.
Then a airthquake come when that was gone
An' swallered the lan' his house stood on.
Then the tax collector he come roun'
An' charged him up for the hole in the groun'.
Then the city marshall he come in view
An' wanted pay for his street tax too.

Did he moan an' sigh? Did he set an' cry?
An' cuss the hurricane sweepin' by?
Did he grieve that his ole friends failed to call
When the airthquake had swallered all?
Never a word of blame he said,
With all them troubles on top his head,
Not him. He clumb to the top of the hill,
Whar standin' room was left him still,
An' barin' his head, here's what he said:
"I reckon it's time to git up and git
But Lord, I ain't had the measles yit!"

This was J. Howard Pew, defiant and recalcitrant to the authorities of the world, but malleable by eternal principles. "Sound principles are eternal—the same yesterday, today, and tomorrow," he would say. And he would summarily reject any compromise between those principles and temporary expedience. In an address to Grove City College Alumni, on April 11, 1949, he put it this way: "I am convinced that our American way of life is being sabotaged by compromise. . . . If you believe in freedom for the individual, you must be opposed to any encroachment of government on the rights of the individual. If you believe that everyone is entitled to the opportunity for an education you cannot believe in government control of that education. If you believe in a free market, you cannot justify government price controls. If these are your principles, they admit no compromise, for you cannot mix right with wrong any more than you can mix contaminated water with pure water without having the whole water contaminated—and it makes no difference how little contaminated water there may be in the mixture."

To J. Howard Pew America was more than merely a home of the homeless all over the earth, it was the land of opportunity for everyone regardless of race or national origin. Of course, this does not mean that you can sit by the roadside and wait for opportunity to come along and invite you for a ride to wealth and influence. You must make your own opportunity as you go along. You do so through work, hard work, and long hours of work. There is no greater asset of any people than the courage and discipline of work, the love of work. For all progress depends on activity, that is, work, whether physical or intellectual. It is no curse, but the evidence of manhood. Howard liked to quote a little poem entitled "Work" by Angela Morgan:

> Work! Thank God for the might of it
> The ardour, the urge, the delight of it—
> Passion of labour daily hurled
> On the mighty anvils of the world.
> Oh, what is so fierce as the flame of it?
> And what is so huge as the aim of it?
> Thundering on through dearth and doubt,
> Calling the plan of the Maker out.

> Work the Titan; Work, the friend,
> Shaping the earth to a glorious end,
> Rending a continent apart
> To answer the dream of the Master heart.
> Thank God for a world where none may shirk!
> Thank God for the splendour of work!

It was hard physical and intellectual labor unleashed by the system of individual enterprise, which, according to J. Howard Pew, made America the most productive country on earth. It has eliminated the poorhouse and further reduced poverty than in any other country. Individual poverty itself is not dishonorable, except when it springs from idleness or intemperance.

The "war on poverty" which the Federal government waged during the 1960's could only breed more poverty as it derided and diminished the value of work and made millions of Americans dependent on government for their existence. It aggravated individual poverty as certain labor laws created mass unemployment, especially among teenagers and minorities. In fact, some Federal laws and policies actually breed institutional poverty through weakening man's incentive to work or denying or destroying the fruits of his labor. According to Mr. Pew, the most ominous of such poverty-breeding policies is inflation, the Federal debauching of our currency. During his lifetime, the purchasing power of the dollar declined some seventy per cent. This meant that savers, pensioners, and other fixed-income recipients lost some seventy per cent of their wealth and income. Inflation indeed has impoverished millions of retired people. Furthermore, government interventions in the form of wage and labor legislation and the legal privileges and immunities granted to the labor unions have greatly hampered industrial productivity. And Federal taxation that prevents the formation of business capital prevents creation of more productive jobs. In short, J. Howard Pew was convinced that certain economic

policies of the Federal government are the most important
single cause of poverty in the United States. He said so on
many occasions.

The decline of freedom in America and the weakening of
its enterprise institutions, as seen by J. Howard Pew, was
not due to alien subversion, but to the apathy and lethargy of
many public leaders and intellectuals. Instead of unequiv-
ocally opposing error and sin, they are condoning and
sanctioning it. "We are constantly being alerted," he warned
in a speech to the Valley Forge Council of Boy Scouts of
America, on January 17, 1953, "to the dangers of subversive
activity at work in our land, but a far greater danger lurks in
what has been termed 'subversive *inactivity*.' No subversive
forces can ever conquer a nation that has not first been con-
quered by 'subversive *inactivity*' on the part of the citizenry,
who have failed in their civic duty and in service to their
country.

"As freedom is our most precious national asset, I am convinced that apathy—indifference—is our greatest national sin.
We have come to take for granted *that* freedom which our
forefathers shed their blood to gain for us."

On other occasions he liked to quote the great Irish pa-
triot, John Philpot Curran:

   The condition under which God hath given liberty to man is
   eternal vigilance, which condition if he break, servitude is at
   once the consequence of his crime and the punishment of his
   guilt.

Pew would then implore his listeners to stand firm in defense
of our liberty and always be mindful that Christianity and liberty are linked together, as are atheism and communism. If
you destroy liberty, Christianity must necessarily be sup-
pressed, as can be observed in all countries behind the Iron
Curtain.

To J. Howard Pew personal liberty, with due regard for the

rights of others, was inexorably tied to Christianity. And political dictatorship that is seeking to enslave man is utterly
incompatible with Christian doctrine. Therefore, in order to
overcome the great dangers of Communism which we are fac-
ing today, there must be a resurgence of Christian faith and
living. If we set a shining example the world may yet be saved,
for we can do more good by being good than in any other
way.

At the Constituting Convention of the National Council of
Churches on December 1, 1950, Mr. Pew expressed his hope for
the world:

"Before we attempt to lead other nations toward peace, we
first must reaffirm our own faith in the moral and spiritual
principles of Christianity, so that we shall be strong enough to
resist the invasion of Communism and other alien influences. Individually and nationally, we must cleanse our
minds of all dishonest thinking. We must strive constantly for
honesty in government, in politics, in business, and in our private lives. We must rededicate ourselves to the service of God,
and be ready at all times to give a 'reason for the faith that
is in us.'

"Then, what is there we can do to stem the onrush of paganism beyond our borders and so avert an ultimate catas-
trophe? I am in difficulty, but I *do* know one thing which we
must *not* do.

"We must not answer hate with hate, lest in setting ourselves up to speak 'with the tongues of men and of angels,'
we seem to become 'as a sounding brass or a tinkling cymbal.'
We may justly hate the crimes of oppression which have been
committed against millions of our fellow human beings, but
we must not fall into the error of transferring our hate to the
victims of those crimes. Somehow we must find ways and
means to develop a Christian, informed public opinion
among the peoples living under dictatorships.

"Which road is the world to take? The road to Christianity

or the road to paganism? There is no other. Here in America, during the last 100 years, the Christian road has provided the world with the greatest spectacle of human progress ever witnessed throughout history. It was achieved only because there was complete religious freedom and a wide-open invitation to all the genius, inventive ability, organizing capacity, and managerial skill of a great people."

Four

●

The Individual Enterprise System

"To me free enterprise is a very noble and simple thing. It connotes the right of the individual to improve his status of life through initiative and hard work. It connotes the right of the consumer to the exercise of free choice as to what and where he should make his purchases. It connotes the right of the worker to exercise a free choice as to where he shall work; and the entrepreneur a free choice as to what business or industry he shall elect to engage in."[*]

IF THE PRESENT STATE of human affairs is the consequence of the past, it is natural to inquire into causes of the good we enjoy and the evils we suffer. For man's history is philosophy teaching by example and by warning.

As a social being man must choose the system of political, social and economic organization that encompasses his life. He must choose between two conceivable alternatives: a system of individual freedom and private property in which free men voluntarily manage their affairs through consent and contract, or a system of cooperation by force. The former is commonly called the private property order, or the market system, the enterprise system, the profit system, capitalism, or laissez-faire. The latter is known by its several historic versions, such as feudalism, mercantilism, socialism, communism, or fascism. There are only these two basic alternatives and the various mixtures of them.

[*]J. Howard Pew Remarks before National Industrial Information Committee, May 10, 1944.

Western civilization, with its early sparks of creative power in ancient Greece, is characterized by short periods of individual freedom and long eras of social coercion. American freedom, as seen by J. Howard Pew, may be traced from Medieval England.

In a speech to The Franklin Institute, on May 17, 1950, he described the evolution:

"The struggle for Anglo-American liberty had its beginnings back in 1215 A.D., when the barons marched their armies down to the banks of the Thames at Runnymede and compelled King John to sign the Magna Charta. Up until that time the peoples of the world had lived under various schemes of government control and economic planning. Their very lives and activities had been subjected to the whims and foibles of their bureaucratic overlords. There were a few brief periods—such as those which obtained in the early development of Greece and of Rome—in which there was established a measure of liberty.

"But with the exception of these brief periods, industry had been conducted on a very elementary scale, largely dominated by the government. The comparatively few people engaged in industry were mostly serfs of the state or industrial slaves. But most of the people not directly employed by the government, were engaged in agriculture, where they struggled with a few hand tools and produced barely sufficient food to eke out an existence for themselves and their families. It can readily be seen, therefore, that under such conditions there existed no field in which management could operate.

"For the next 500 years there was a perpetual quarrel between the kings and the Parliament. During certain periods Parliament would succeed in exercising a measure of control over the king; and during other periods the king would make Parliament subservient to his wishes. But it made little difference whether the Parliament or the king controlled the state—

in both cases the lives and activities of the people were subjected to bureaucratic controls. During most of this period the state controlled commodities, prices and wages. Certain rulers—such as Queen Elizabeth—made a practice of rewarding their court favorites by giving them an absolute monopoly on such necessities as salt, iron, oil, beer, and a vast number of other articles of commerce.

"But in the eighteenth century the Anglo-American people demanded and progressively received more and more freedom at the hands of their rulers. Under the stimulus of freedom many new institutions came into being, the most important of which was the free market. And just as the free market grew and developed, to that extent the scope and responsibility of management did likewise. Just as the market became freer, to that extent management had a larger area in which to exercise its genius, initiative, ability, organizing capacity and managerial skill. Management by its very nature has always been inexorably tied to the free market. The one never could exist without the other.

"The latter part of the eighteenth century found the American Colonists leading the fight for liberty. Many of the leaders among the Colonists had come to America in order to escape tyranny at home—but they found that England was exploiting the American Colonies to a point where manufacturing was well-nigh impossible. The Colonists were compelled to export their raw materials to England, where they were manufactured into finished products. They were also compelled to import goods manufactured in England. When to these prohibitions were added many vexatious taxes, such as that on sugar, on tea, and those imposed by affixing stamps, the ministers from their pulpits, the editors in their papers, and the lawyers in town meetings, stirred the people up by pointing out the injustices to which they were being subjected. The Revolution followed.

"Then in 1787 came the Constitution of the United States—

the greatest charter of liberty ever penned by the hand of man. The framers of this great document believed that the only useful purpose to be served by government was that of guaranteeing to its people life, liberty and the pursuit of happiness. They knew that political office conferred power on the recipient but that wisdom was acquired by quite a different process. They were determined that a man either elected or appointed to public office should not exercise that power to impair their freedom. Into that document they put positive limitations on all governmental power and specified that any power not expressly given to the Federal Government remained with the individual citizens and their local state governments. Freedom of the market place then became the accepted order."

In this free market order, competition—the striving of individuals to excel in the service of others in order to gain personal wealth and position—is a powerful driving force. It causes manufacturers and merchants to outdo one another by providing better or cheaper goods and services. J. Howard Pew welcomed competition which to him was an incentive that inspired people to maximize output, to exercise the utmost of their genius, inventive ability, organizing capacity and managerial skill. And, according to Pew, it affords industrial peace and harmony. "It is the only urge which induces the industrial workers and the investors to coordinate their interests and strive for a common objective—production." In an article published in *The National Petroleum News* (May 2, 1945) he wrote:

"The competitive enterprise system in America, based on pleasing the customer, has provided greater incentive to economic and technological progress than any other system, and in a short period of little more than 150 years has given us the highest standard of living ever achieved by any country at any time in the world's history. I have a strong and fervent faith in the continuing superiority of our competitive enterprise system to expand our economy and to provide employment for all who are able and willing to work."

Economists favor the abolition of all trade barriers so that people may compete on the market. Such barriers protect the less efficient businessman from his more efficient rival. They perpetuate backward technology and methods of production. And, above all, they cause production to shift from favorable locations to places that are less efficient and productive. In short, trade restrictions hamper economic output and thus impair living conditions, no matter whether the restrictions take the form of special privileges, government monopolies, labor unions, or cartels.

Throughout his long life J. Howard Pew encountered the restrictive policies of cartels and struggled uncompromisingly for his independence. In a speech to the directors of the Guaranty Trust Company of New York, on April 18, 1945, he described his experience:

"We had a dominating position in the German market, which enabled us to keep as much German business as we wanted—until Hitler came into power. One of his first acts was to force us into the oil cartel; and from that moment mandates were piled on mandates, controls on controls, restrictions on restrictions, compulsions on compulsions—until there was no consideration which would justify our continuance of this business, and so we sold out to one of our competitors. The same thing happened in France and Italy; and when the present war broke out, the English Government notified us that we must join their cartel. My answer was to close our shop, dispose of the stocks, and bring the staff home. And so I have learned about cartels in the school of bitter experience.

"Now I should like to give you my definition of cartels. It is not the definition to be found in Webster's dictionary, nor is it the specious definition sometimes advanced by selfish interests; but it is truly representative of the way in which these cartels have operated in Europe for the last thirty years. They fall into three classes:

"First is the private cartel, which is an agreement entered into by two or more independent enterprises for the purpose of fixing prices, controlling production, or allocating territory. As such, it is the acme of bad sportsmanship and a conspiracy against the consuming public.

"Then comes the Government cartel, which is the private cartel conducted under the aegis of Government; Government, however, undertaking to compel its nationals to join the cartel.

"Finally there is the super-state cartel, which is an agreement entered into by two or more countries for the purpose of fixing prices, controlling production, or allocating territory; the contracting countries, however, agreeing to compel their nationals to join the cartel.

"The private cartel represents monopolistic practices in restraint of trade, which have been outlawed in our country for over fifty years. The reprehensible and evil nature of these practices is beyond dispute. Their effect has been to destroy initiative, close the door of opportunity to the new individual enterpreneur, destroy small business units, raise prices, and thus reduce the standard of living. These fruits of the cartel system result in the freezing of progress, which is to the detriment of the consumers, the workers, and those with savings to invest. Few voices today are raised in defense of the so-called private cartel; but there is a school of thought which believes that an undertaking which is against the public interest —and thus bad—can be purified and made good if it be conducted under the aegis of Government.

"The Government cartel is far more reprehensible than the private cartel because it contains all the evils of the private cartel without any means by which it can be eradicated. Ever since the New Deal came into power, they have surreptitiously endeavored to devise some means by which they could bring all business and industry under the absolute control of the Government. They early realized that if business and industry could be forced into cartels, then the Government could take over the control. The NRA was the first abortive effort to accomplish this purpose. It was providential that the Supreme Court at that time had the courage to declare the NRA unconstitutional; just as it was providential, a few days ago, when Mr. Byrnes had the courage to expose the deceptive nature of the National Service Act. I am wondering whether Providence will interfere to save us from the so-called trade accords. The super-state cartel represents a new evolution in the cartel idea, under the deceptive label of trade accords."

J. Howard Pew agreed with market economists that free trade benefits all the peoples of the world and therefore is desirable. But he refused to draw the obvious conclusion that all trade restrictions, including the protective tariff must be disapproved and abolished. In a dramatic encounter with his fellow-trustees of the Foundation for Economic Education, Inc., on December 5, 1960, he pleaded his case for protective tariffs. "Free trade is impossible so long as most of the countries of the world manipulate the value of their money and the rate of their exchanges.

"Free trade is impossible so long as most of the countries of the world permit state cartels, super-state cartels, and private cartels.

"Free trade cannot exist so long as dictators in a large percentage of the countries of the world fix the price of their export goods.

"Free trade is influenced to a very large extent by the internal tax policies imposed by the different countries of the world.

"These and many other barriers to free trade imposed by nations—nations selfishly motivated by a desire to put their nationals in an advantageous position as compared with the nationals of other countries—must all be eliminated before free trade can be made to function. The tariff might well be regarded as a defense mechanism, rather than as a barrier to free trade."

He also argued that lower labor costs in foreign countries handicap American competition, that low ocean freight rates have brought foreign industries very close to our shores, that U.S. capital, technology and know-how was exported since the war and is "now preparing to destroy our economy," and finally that a policy of tariff reductions must be seen as a supplementary effort to the costly foreign aid program that is serving the "one-world philosophy." In short, free trade would "permit foreign manufacturers to drive domestic manufacturers out of business."

At the Foundation, a well-known bastion of individual freedom and free trade, many trustees were puzzled by his arguments, which seemed at variance with his usual distrust in governmental ability to protect American industry. Surely, they argued, the world economy is laboring hard under a maze of world-wide trade restrictions. But are we to imitate the bad examples set by other countries, or should we strive to offer a shining example of freedom to the rest of the world? Also, who is best qualified to cope with harmful trade restrictions, the American businessman, or bureaucrats and politicians? Hourly labor costs, indeed, are higher in the U.S., but it is the unit costs of production that determine the competitive position. Equipped with massive capital at relatively low interest costs, American industry may actually produce at lower unit costs and, therefore enjoy a competitive advantage. If U.S. foreign aid leads to distortions and maladjustments in foreign trade, would it not be more judicious to reduce or abolish that aid rather than entrust government with a new power over business? In the eyes of some FEE trustees, Mr. Pew presented arguments for tariff protection merely to learn their views and answers to the traditional position of most American industrialists.

If competition is the driving force that induces men to outdo one another by providing better and cheaper goods and services, it is the tools of production, i.e. capital, that may determine the outcome of the race. Wage rates depend on productivity which in turn is largely determined by the amount of capital invested per head of the population. America is the richest country on earth because the amount of capital per worker is the largest on earth. J. Howard Pew taught this fundamental lesson of economic reality on countless occasions, as when he lectured before a company sales group meeting in Philadelphia:

"Prosperity, we have all been taught to believe, is something to be desired—and so it is. But let us see if we can define it. Some people believe prosperity means full employment; others that it means a higher standard of living; and others that it means a higher national income, better schools, better this or better that. But the truth is that prosperity is none of these. Prosperity means prosperous business. When business is prosperous then better living, more employment and higher incomes for workers, managers and industrialists is the inevitable result. Now, it is production that makes prosperity possible. The more goods that are produced, the greater is our prosperity. When I talk about production, I refer not only to taking the oil out of the ground, transporting and refining it, but also everything which is necessary to deliver that oil into the hands of the consumer.

"This all becomes quite clear to me when I think of what would happen if, say, six able-bodied men were cast upon a deserted island. Obviously they would all have to go to work or perish. Undoubtedly each would be assigned a job for which he was best fitted. One might be a fisherman, two would probably be farmers, one a hunter, one a cook, and the sixth might be assigned the job of providing shelter. Now suppose one of these men happened to be a witch doctor who professed to believe that the less they worked the better they would be provided for, the higher would be their standard of living. Certainly the other five would tolerate no such nonsense.

"It is just as simple as that. But these witch doctors constantly confuse us by talking about money and banking, as though money and banking could produce anything. In its proper place, money and banking is useful because it enables us more easily to exchange the goods we produce for the goods which other people produce.

"Prehistoric man lived scarcely better than did the animals. Then the hammer was invented, which enabled him to build a better shelter for himself. Then the bow and arrow enabled him to obtain meat. Then gradually one tool after another was developed. Later he learned to operate these tools with oxen and horses. With this development civilization advanced rapidly and was still further accelerated when water power, steam, electricity and the internal combustion engine came into general use.

"Now there is a wide variety of tools. First there were the primary tools, such as the saw and the hammer, the bucket and the wheelbarrow. Then there were the tools which are operated by means other than those of manpower, such as the plow and all the tools commonly found in machine shops, boiler shops, carpenter shops, and the like. Finally there are the plants themselves, such as our refinery, in which crude oil is refined into gasoline and other petroleum products. Another illustration is the flour mill, where wheat is made into flour; or the sulphuric acid plant, where brimstone, or pyrites, is converted into sulphuric acid. All such plants are today regarded as tools. Thus any device used for the purpose of changing one material into another is called a tool.

"The cost of tools averages between five and seven thousand dollars for every industrial worker in America. In the oil industry, that cost is fifteen thousand dollars. Just think of it—for every man and woman employed in the oil industry, there is an investment in tools of fifteen thousand dollars. Now these investors should receive a reasonable rental for the use of the tools which they have provided; otherwise, they will not be able to save up sufficient money with which to replace the old ones when they become obsolete, or to buy new tools for the new workers. Those whom industry employ as operators should do everything possible to make them produce the maximum products which they are capable of turning out, because, if for any reason these employees are prevented either from using the most modern tools or from operating those tools at their maximum capacity, then their wages and salaries as measured by their standard of living will either have to be reduced or, at best, remain stationary— and that is not the way to obtain prosperity."

All factors of production are equally important in the final result. No one can rise from want and poverty without the unremitting efforts of all members of society—workers, managers and investors. Management, capital and labor must combine together for common effort. To illustrate the importance of cooperation Mr. Pew liked to tell this story:

"There is a legendary story about an old Arab. This old Arab had three sons. Realizing that he had but a short time to live, and being desirous of ascertaining which of his three sons should succeed him as head of the family, he called them together and told them that in a distant land were a group of scientists who had developed some amazing things; and then he instructed them to this effect: They were to journey together until they arrived at this distant land, and then they were to separate and spend six months in search for the acquisition of a present, the nature of the present to be such as would contribute most to the old Arab's welfare. At the end of the six months they were to meet at the place where they had entered the distant land and journey home together.

At the end of the six months they met as planned and immediately displayed the presents which they had acquired. One had bought a magic carpet on which could be transported a number of people at an amazing speed; another a magic medicine which would cure any ill; and the third a magic glass through which could be seen that which transpired in any home throughout the world. They then turned the glass on their father's home and were dismayed to find that the old Arab was ill unto death. So they jumped onto the magic carpet, were quickly transported to their father's home, where the magic medicine was administered and the old Arab's life was saved.

"Which of the three sons contributed most to the old Arab's welfare? Obviously the contribution of no one was of any real value without that of the other two; and the contribution of no two without that of the other one.

"And so it is with labor, management and capital. In our modern economy no one of these can accomplish anything worthwhile without that of the other two."

If cooperation is the essence of the individual enterprise system, free prices are the regulators of commerce and industry. There is no need for an economic czar or central controller; millions of prices voluntarily agreed to by buyers and sellers regulate economic transactions better than any committee of wise planners ever could. Free prices keep demand and supply in continuous equilibrium and guide the process of production. In fact, there is no more important pillar of the free enterprise system than the freedom of economic exchanges at free prices.

From his background of experience and knowledge of economics, J. Howard Pew frequently lectured on the basic principles of price and price controls. At a meeting of the Empire State Petroleum Association, on April 11, 1946, he gave this lecture:

"Free prices are the regulators of American industry. They

control the volume of production; they shift savings to where they are needed; they move workers into fields of production in greatest demand. They give consumers what they want.

"There is no substitute for free prices. Government directives cannot do the job in peacetime for the simple reason that neither a few men, nor even several hundred thousand can take the place of the day-by-day functioning of a free market reflecting the judgment and desires of 100,000,000 consumers.

"That is the answer to those who say price control is all right if O.P.A. administered the law fairly. Price control cannot be made fair because it is physically impossible for O.P.A. to work out equitable price relationships. Let me demonstrate:

"We have in this country some 8,000,000 articles of trade. We have 140 metropolitan marketing areas. The number of equations necessary to establish proper price relationships in the metropolitan marketing areas would be 140 times 8,000,000 or 1,120,000,000. We have some 50,000,000 workers whose wage rates might be reduced for convenience to 1,000 classifications. To establish proper wage-price relationships the number of equations would be 1,000 times 1,120,000,000 or 1,120,000,000,000—one trillion one hundred and twenty billion equations! Computing one equation an hour, it would require the 50,000,000 workers in America ten years to do the job working 40 hours a week, with only one week off a year for vacation!

"Of course, it is fantastic! So the price fixers resort to formulas for universal application, freezing prices to some previous level. But no sooner are such formulas proclaimed than conditions change. American business cannot be operated by formulas. If it could, it would have been figured out years ago and all business enterprises would be successful while their managers could go on year-long vacations.

"But, say the O.P.A. propagandists in another specious

argument: 'Price increases cause inflation; inflation helps none but hurts everyone; O.P.A. keeps down prices, and thus is the only barrier standing between the country and a devastating inflation.'

"This is double talk designed to deceive and confuse. It is putting the cart before the horse. Price increases no more cause inflation than wet streets cause rain. Wet streets are a result of rain and rising prices are one of the many disastrous results that follow in the wake of inflation.

"Inflation results from an expansion in purchasing power that is not matched by a comparable expansion in the production of real consumer goods and services. We have an inflationary condition today as a result of the monetizing of the Federal debt, and war accumulated shortages in certain consumer goods, aggravated by O.P.A. controls.

"The only effective ways to halt this inflationary trend are to balance the Federal Budget this year and to stimulate the production of goods that people want by taking the O.P.A. off the backs of business and industry."

At other times Mr. Pew spoke as an economic historian who cited interesting lessons of history:

"A Chinese writer on Confucius describes price fixing and manipulation of supply and demand as early as the fifth century B.C. In a town where he lived a superintendent was appointed for each shop, and prices were rigidly fixed. For every 20 shops there was a master of merchants to fix the prices. It was decreed that even in the time of crop failure and famine grain should be sold at the same prices that normally prevailed. The scheme necessitated an army of government officials, inspectors, overseers and other functionaries just as governmental planning has multiplied our public officials. An auditor of price was required, to see that the merchants adhered to the government-fixed prices; but the government attempted to control supplies by raising or lowering prices. A central bank was set up, similar to our Federal financial agencies, to buy up crop surpluses and to hold them until they could be fed out at the prices which the government had fixed. Because of the impossibility of administering such a program, police became an important part of the marketing plan. The gate to the market place was guarded by two policemen with whips and halberds. Every two shops had a policeman on guard and for every ten shops there was a captain of police. Finally, a detective was assigned to every five shops, whose duty it was to spy on all the others. Eventually the excessively high cost of living under the plan became intolerable. The story of the resultant riots, demoralization, suffering and disaster is too long to recount. Anyhow, whether as a means to obtain reasonable prices or to build up a huge political machine, the entire scheme was a miserable failure.

"Rome under Augustus reached its climax of prosperity. Augustus was no economic planner. Under his regime commerce and trade were given pretty free sway. But most of the later emperors went in strong for planning. The government tried to run practically everything. The senate gradually surrendered most of its powers to the emperor, but the process was not nearly so rapid as was the abdication of Congressional authority in this country during the present administration. By the time of Diocletian, in the third century, things had become altogether bad. The economic planners had, by favoring the cheaper agriculture of the provinces, well-nigh destroyed the agriculture of Italy. Finally, Diocletian took things firmly in hand and inaugurated a new deal. He decreed that half of all the existing vineyards should be destroyed; that a subsidy should be paid for increased production of grain; that the prices of goods and services should be rigidly fixed; and that heavy penalties should be imposed for all violations.

"The story of that Egyptian Pharaoh whom Joseph served, as told in the book of Genesis, may well be referred to here in the light of our country's recent experiments. When the famine fell upon Egypt, Pharaoh, who had already stored vast quantities of grain, gathered up all the money in the land and brought the money into Pharaoh's house—just as our economic planners several years ago gathered up all of our gold. Then Pharaoh, having control of both the money and the food, put the people on relief and fed them, incidentally taking all of their cattle. And when he got tired of feeding them and they came back for more food, he gave them food in exchange for their land. Next he removed the people from the land and herded them in the cities. (A resettlement program!) Finally, he made a seed distribution and sent the people back to the land as his tenants, exacting one-fifth of all their produce as rent. Now, that may seem a bit steep; but it is really quite moderate as compared with the cost of our government, which for the last five years has averaged over 27 per cent of the national income, which is almost one-half more than that which Pharaoh exacted." (From an address delivered to the Salesmanship Club of Dallas, February 9, 1939).

J. Howard Pew combined judgment with wit to express his thought. His parables, poems and rhymes helped to say much in few words and gave his speeches a flavor that was his very own. The favorite target for his shaft of wit was the central planner who would replace individual freedom with government authority. In a speech to the Men's League of the Marble Church in New York City, on May 11, 1948, he explained the "lightning bug" approach:

"Those who seek to establish a collectivist state and impose a dictated economy upon the people seem to get their inspiration from failures. Confucius is regarded as one of the wisest men of all ages, but the fact that he abandoned his plan to control the lives of the people seems to have made no impression upon succeeding generations. Generation after generation of would-be planners have looked to the past for their ideas, regardless of the fact that never has a dictated,

controlled economy worked. They make one think of the low-
ly lightning bug which someone has characterized thus:

> The lightning bug is brilliant
> 　But it hasn't any mind,
> It travels through existence
> 　With its headlight on behind.

"The most recent attempt to try this lightning bug approach to a planned economy is being made by our friends
the British. They seem to have utterly forsaken the teachings
of their great statesman, Edmund Burke, who more than 150
years ago warned that 'The people never give up their liber-
ties except under some delusion.' It is now a common saying
in London that Government control has become Britain's biggest industry. Under their present Labor socialist Government 25,000 rules and regulations control the life of every
British man, woman and child. The following story will illustrate the absurdities to which such a controlled economy
leads. As you know, the British are justly proud of their Angus cattle. Recently the English Board of Trade issued an
edict that metal discs be attached to the horns of pedigreed
Angus bulls to be exported. Later this order was amended
and another edict issued that the horns of Angus bulls to be
exported should be branded. Later this edict was revoked
entirely because the Board of Trade discovered that Angus
bulls don't have horns at all.

"The would-be controllers in our own country have now
developed a well-ordered technique by which they hope the
evolution from a free country to a totalitarian state can be effected. It is very simple. First, a few innocuous controls—at
the end of the year the public, realizing that they did not
work, protest—the controllers readily agree and point out
that the reason they did not work was because the controls
didn't go far enough—so the lawmaking bodies provide more
controls—at the end of the next year they go through the
same procedures—are given more controls—until at the end of

six or eight years they have succeeded in getting from the Government the absolute right to dominate the lives and activities of the people.

"Now, the American people do not want a totalitarian state. Repeated polls of public opinion confirm this. They believe in our American way of life, but they don't understand the processes by which the product of our American life has been effectuated."

Mr. Pew would convey his thought by comparison or occasionally refer to authority to prove his point. In a speech to the Grove City College Alumni he cited the Hoover Report:

"As you know, some time ago the President appointed a Commission, headed by ex-President Hoover, to make a study of our Federal Government and then make recommendations as to how it could be streamlined. This Commission has now finished its study and from the Hoover report I would like to present some facts, as they should have a direct bearing on any consideration of socialized medicine which is so much in the public mind today. To begin with, the Hoover Commission found the Federal Government was composed of 1,800 separate bureaus and agencies. Of these, 40 different agencies are giving medical care to an estimated 24,000,000 beneficiaries—about one-sixth of the population—at a minimum cost of more than $2 billion. These 40 agencies operate under different authorities, and follow different policies. They compete for doctors, hospitals and funds with, as the Commission states, 'no regard for the needs of others.' There seems to be no declaration of Government policy as to who is eligible to receive free Government medical care, nor who is to give it. There prevails the usual bureaucratic thirst for power, inefficiency and waste. The construction cost of the various hospital-building agencies the Commission found ranged from $20,000 up to $51,000 per bed, whereas the average per bed cost in private voluntary hospitals is only $16,000 per bed. Within the past year there were 255,000 Government hospital beds available for 155,000 patients, all this at a time when the Veterans Administration was planning an additional 38,000 beds. The Commission adds that the Federal Agencies do not make effective use of their physician personnel; some doctors are overworked while others are practically idle. In the face of this factual report do you think anyone should be censured for not wanting to turn our entire medical profession over to the Federal Government? However, this presents only the administrative and material side of the picture. There is an issue of far deeper significance to be considered in the socialization of medicine. The Governmental mind is slavishly devoted to established forms and accepted precedents and persistently hostile to innovation, experiment and research which make for progress. Men of vision have had to work unceasingly for the emancipation of the human intellect from such restrictions. It has remained for a comparatively small group of rare spirits, inspired by genius and daring to bring American medicine and surgery to its present high estate."

J. Howard Pew could never get used to the thought that the numerous production restrictions which government imposed were designed to improve the national welfare. He could not understand how the production restrictions on food, for instance, the quotas, subsidies for output reduction, the Federal destruction of some crops in the field, the soil bank program, and huge give-aways could be for the "social good," "social welfare," or "social justice." To him this was sheer quackery:

"Fakirs and quacks surround us. We find them in every phase of human activity, but the economic quacks outnumber all the rest. These quack economists would have us believe that they could cure all of our business ills in no time at all. They are like the quack doctor who was asked to sit in consultation with a group of real doctors. After the prospect had been put through his examination, one of the doc-

tors announced that the patient was convalescing. 'Ah,'
spoke up the quack doctor, 'that isn't serious. I've often
cured that in 24 hours.'

"These quack economists would have us believe that the
Government ought to plan everything for us and control all
our activities. They believe that if we would only produce
less, all of us would be better provided for. This happy theory so impressed Ogden Nash that he wrote a little poem,
'One From One Leaves Two.' Let me try to repeat it. It runs:

> Higgledy piggledy, my black hen,
> She lays eggs for gentlemen.
> Gentlemen come every day
> To count what my black hen doth lay.
> If perchance she lays too many,
> They fine my hen a pretty penny;
> If perchance she fails to lay
> The gentlemen a bonus pay.
>
> Mumbledy pumbledy, my red cow,
> She's cooperating now.
> At first she didn't understand
> That milk production must be planned;
> She didn't understand at first
> She either had to plan or burst,
> But now, the Government reports,
> She's giving pints instead of quarts.
>
> Fiddle-de-dee, my next-door neighbors,
> They are giggling at their labors.
> First they plant the tiny seed,
> Then they water, then they weed,
> Then they hoe and prune and lop,
> Then they raise a record crop,
> Then they laugh their sides asunder,
> And plow the whole kaboodle under.
>
> Abracadabra, thus we learn
> The more you create, the less you earn,
> The less you earn, the more you're given,
> The less you lead, the more you're driven.
> The more destroyed, the more they feed,

> The more you pay, the more they need,
> The more you earn, the less you keep,
> And now I lay me down to sleep.

"Our American system of free enterprise is far more than just a way of doing business. It is a system which at its best comprehends good sportsmanship; gives free play to the law of supply and demand and of competition; produces an ever-increasing standard of living; develops initiative, character, and discipline; and in many ways goes far toward improving the morale and bettering the lives of our people." (From a speech to the annual Congress of American Industry, on December 12, 1940.)

Since its inception on January 1, 1937, the Social Security program undoubtedly has become the most sacred welfare institution in the country. Through it, government dispenses to nearly thirty million elderly Americans a monthly allowance that is to assure them decent living conditions in retirement. Over the years the program has become the most significant welfare and redistribution scheme, as benefits are no longer determined by the contributions made by the recipients, but rather by government considerations of fairness and adequacy. It has become a political football that is tossed around by the politicians of both political parties in their bids for the votes of the elderly. In preparation for national elections, benefit improvements are usually granted regardless of the contributions made in the past. It taxes the working population for the benefit of a growing number of retirees. In particular, it extracts ever larger contributions from businessmen and professional people whose benefits begin only at age 72 on account of certain income restrictions. But the life expectancy of the American male is only 67, which means that few businessmen and professionals live long enough to collect their benefits. Undoubtedly the Social Security program, to which medical care was later added, is

engaged in the greatest redistribution of wealth ever under-
taken in the history of the world.

To criticize the system is sheer political folly. The only
criticism that may be heard today is its "insufficiency," it is
not going far enough. In utter disregard of the popularity of
the system, J. Howard Pew opposed it on principle. To him
the Social Security program meant massive redistribution,
economic decline and moral corruption, leading to inflation
and monetary destruction. He liked to tell the parable of the
wild duck, written by the great Danish philosopher, Kierke-
gaard:

"With his mates this duck was flying in the springtime
northward across Europe. During the flight he came down in a
Danish barnyard where there were tame ducks. He ate of
their corn and he liked it. He stayed for an hour—then for a
day—then a week—then a month—and finally, because he rel-
ished the good fare and the safety of the barnyard, he stayed
all summer. Then one autumn day when the flock of wild
ducks were winging their way southward again, they passed
over the barnyard and their mate heard their cry. His breast
stirred with a strange thrill of joy and delight and, with a
great flapping of wings, he rose in the air to join his old com-
rades in their flight—but he found his good fare had made him
fat and his muscles so soft and flabby that he could rise no
higher than the eaves of the barn. So he dropped back into
the barnyard and said to himself, 'Oh, well, my life is safe
here and the food is good.' But, alas, he was not safe from
the man who fed him, for he later discovered that he was
being fattened for the kill.

"I have every sympathy with the lot of the worker. And I
venture to boast that I know of no group of employees who
enjoy as steady employment or more liberal health insurance,
thrift and benefit plans than that provided by our Company.
. . . I am convinced that the OASI program constitutes the
greatest threat to our enterprise system of any Federal mea-

sure. I call it the greatest threat to enterprise, because inherent in this scheme is further inflation and the destruction of the character of individuals, either of which leads to disaster.

"The history of all old age benefit plans established by other countries in the past, has been that payments progressively increased and age limits were constantly lowered, until eventually they could no longer be borne by the state.

"Politicians fall into the snare because they realize that payments during the earlier years are not too large, and, as they do not expect to be here when the critical time comes, they just let the future take care of itself. . . .

"The men who in 1787 wrote the Constitution of the United States, were keen students of economic history. Men in political life today rarely possess such knowledge. In fact, few men in any walk of life are conversant with the economic conditions which implemented important events in history, for our modern histories largely confine their writings to the exploits of warriors and politicians.

"But in 1787 the educated classes knew the historical significance of the 'Society of Status' and the 'Society of Contract'; that the one was the very antithesis of the other. They knew that the 'Society of Status' comprehended the all-powerful state under which the status of the individual was little more than that of the serf; that most men had lived under such a status for many centuries.

"Knowing that those who live best produce most, and believing this could be effected only when men were free to exercise their initiative, ingenuity and resourcefulness—our forebears were determined that they should create for this country a political atmosphere which would be conducive to the development of an economy based on the 'Society of Contract'.

"While an economy based on the 'Society of Contract' had never been entirely effected in any European country, nevertheless the educated people in 1787 had observed that to the extent it had been used, just to that extent the people were happier and their countries more prosperous.

"Anyone reading the Constitution, the Bill of Rights, and the Declaration of Independence—keeping in mind meanwhile the philosophy of the 'Society of Contract'—will be impressed with the fidelity with which they adhere to that philosophy.

"All forms of planned, dictated economies—such as Socialism, Communism, Fascism, and so forth—have only one alluring thing to sell to the people which the 'Society of Contract' apparently lacks, and that is so-called Social Security. Controllers throughout the world contend that pensions for all men, regardless of whether they need or deserve them, is a great moral issue, social justice, progressive, humanitarian, a right of man. But, as a matter of fact, it is none of these, for it is unjust, regressive, immoral, anti-social. Nature has done a pretty good job in developing our animal kingdom, yet not one creature has nature provided with real security.

"The 'Society of Contract' does not guarantee to provide for all the wants of the individual from the womb to the tomb; but it does provide opportunity for men to exercise their talents and thus provide for themselves a degree of happiness and a scale of living far beyond that of the mere subsistence provided by the 'Society of Status.' Just as soon as an individual ceases to depend on his own resources, he develops the psychology of the serf. He has now become conditioned as a fit subject for the all-powerful state.

"It is freedom that has released the energies of individuals, with the result that our economy has developed as has no other in the world's history.

"Government promise of Social Security is a fraud, because the Government has nothing excepting only that which it takes from the people, and there is no feasible way by which it could create a reserve. Government promise of Social Security is by its very nature an uneconomic measure because it destroys freedom, and freedom is the foundation of our economy. Government promise of Social Security is a phony, a hoax, and would never have been accepted by the people of this country excepting only for the sophistry practiced by our economic and political witch doctors.

"Dr. H. W. Griffith, formerly a practicing minister of the gospel, appeared before the Ways and Means Committee last April and made out a devastating case against Social Security. Among other things, he said: 'Real Social Security will come from only one thing: increased and further increased production. This will automatically carry with it full employment, steady employment, and a wider diffusion of economic good. Nothing else will provide these things. Prosperity, like happiness, is never achieved when sought for itself. It is always a by-product, gained only when men seek first of all to be useful, to find and to satisfy real economic needs.'

"Let me here quote from Mr. Howard E. Kershner, one of the leaders of the Society of Friends: 'Countless numbers of old people who, after a lifetime of industry and thrift, considered their old age secure, now find themselves in want, with greatly reduced or vanished incomes as a result of these destructive and wasteful policies of the economic saviors. Formerly, prudent and thrifty people could be sure of security in old age as a result of their own savings. Now the policy of the Government results in devaluing their savings, reducing their incomes, increasing the cost of living, and destroying the peace and security which they have earned by a lifetime of effort. Today fear and insecurity is more wide-spread than ever before. We are distributing poverty and not wealth. We are taking from those who have, without bettering the condition of those who have not. We are slowly creating mass poverty instead of mass abundance, and we have placed the premium upon irresponsible, shiftless, spendthrift living, rather than upon sober, industrious, thrifty and economical living. A man who denies himself, saves and accumulates all his life, can look forward to having his property taken from him for the benefit of the shiftless, indolent wastrel.'

"In his book, *There's Freedom for the Brave,* Paul McGuire, the Australian political economist, historian and lecturer, writes: 'Bismarck understood that the propertyless masses of the new economy could be regimented with ease once they had swallowed Social Security. If they became dependent on the State, the State could depend on them. No better means have yet been devised for containing the worker than a Social Security card. It soothes him with glib promises; and it gives the State and its status quo an immediate hold on him. The industrial worker whose daily bread comes to him under political guarantees and disciplines learns to curb his indignation at the never-ending audacity of elected persons and their bureaucratic tools.'

"How has it been possible to impose such economic quackery on the American people as this so-called Social Security? The answer seems to be:

"(1) Politicians seize upon it because it enables them to give more gratuities to more people. Plutarch said that he who first gave gratuities to the Roman people was he who was responsible for the fall of the Roman Empire.

"(2) the masses accept it because they have been falsely told that they will thereby obtain something that they would not otherwise receive.

"(3) Some businessmen accept it because they hope thereby to escape their responsibility to provide pensions which their employees have earned.

"The real issue therefore is: Shall we destroy our American economy and everybody with it, in order to attempt the impossible by giving everyone security?

"Great Britain claims that Social Security is the answer to the problem of destitution and still keep the enterprise system intact; but in this they are mistaken. Social Security and other kindred measures of so-called social reform have reduced England to the status of a Socialistic State—and

Socialism is only a way station on the road to a totalitarian state. In England today there are only 45 individuals left with spendable incomes in excess of $24,000.

"Now saving is an economic necessity. Savings of the middle class, while small, are invested in bonds, life insurance, and so forth. But it is new venture capital that is needed. An economy which stifles them is bound to stagnate and decay, for individuals who would provide such venture capital would be eliminated in favor of the Government. Social Security will therefore, if introduced on a large scale, bring the whole national economy under the control of the Government. It is not a substitute for, but a direct road to Socialism." (Remarks at an NAM meeting, on October 26, 1949).

As Chairman of the Board, Mr. Pew gave a similar speech to the faculty of Grove City College, his alma mater. But in spite of his pleading, all the members of administration and faculty, except for the three economists, voted to join the system. For the old faculty members close to retirement age the temptation soon to draw benefits without having contributed much to the system was overwhelming. To J. Howard Pew the vote was a bitter disappointment.

As Mr. Pew had anticipated at the inception of the Social Security System, the taxes that are levied on workers' income have risen steadily since 1937. From a revenue of $387 million in fiscal 1938 the System grew to extract $48.6 billion in 1971, the year of his death. Social insurance taxes rose to become the most onerous tax after the individual income tax and will soon exceed it. (Estimated 1975 receipts: $85.6 billion from SI taxes vs. $129.0 billion from individual income taxes.) It rose from 2 per cent of $3000 income in 1937 to 10.4 per cent of $7,800 income in 1971; and to 11.7 per cent of an ever-higher minimum income since then. It is rising rapidly and must be expected to reach rates and burdens of taxation similar to those of the older European systems of Social Security.

To J. Howard Pew all taxes levied to redistribute income

and wealth meant economic destruction and moral decay.
His analysis of the effects of the ever-rising burden of taxation was irrefutable. "When the government confiscates that
which the savers have accumulated," he discoursed before
the Associated Industries of the Quad-Cities in Davenport,
Iowa, on September 24, 1953, "society suffers grievously in
at least three important respects:

1. By breaking down of the morals of the people.
2. By preventing the savers from purchasing the tools of production.
3. By denying to society the ingenuity and resourcefulness of
   those rare individuals who, like Henry Ford, understood
   how to use tools in order to best supply the needs of the
   American people.

"It is well to consider what has taken place in England.
Years ago they conceived the idea that, if they could only
confiscate the wealth of the people and let the Government
operate industry, England would prosper. How well they
have succeeded in confiscating the wealth of the people, is
evidenced by the fact that in 1939 there were 8,000 people
in Great Britain who had an income of $30,000 per year after
taxes. In 1951 there were only 60 individuals in Great Britain
with incomes after taxes of $16,800; and in 1952 the num-
ber had fallen to 39. They have destroyed their 'seed corn.'
Government has made a failure of their operation of industry—as Governments always do—and there are no longer people in Great Britain who have money to invest in enterprise.
We are following the same road that England took a few
years ago. Can we retrace our steps?

"What kind of a future is in store for the young men of today who possess character, initiative, leadership, and a willingness to work—those qualities which brought success in our
generation? Can these young men be inspired to do their best,
when they know that the State will confiscate all or a large
part of their corporate earnings; and then that income taxes

will extract all or most of what is left; and finally that inheritance taxes will mop up what may have escaped the other two operations?

"Twenty odd years ago the American people believed that when an individual created something everybody was benefited. That, too, was the attitude of the Government. What has brought about a change? The answer seems to be:

"Twenty years ago the great objective of the American people was freedom—the Government being primarily an organization set up by the people to act as its servant to protect that freedom. Gradually during these intervening years the Government is coming to be the State; and the people are coming to be the servants of the State. Those persons who now control the State exercise power over a huge bureaucracy of 2½ millions of people—each one a potential propagandist. They manage the funds with which millions upon millions of voters are subsidized. They control giant corporations. The great political parties are not quarreling with each other over the elimination of these powers; but rather are they competing for the right to wield them.

"Our Federal bureaucracy has increased fivefold in 20 years. Resort is had to every known device to increase the size and power of that bureaucracy. One emergency after another has been created. Each time State power has increased, individual freedom decreased. This is not new in statecraft. In 1794, James Madison wrote about:

> The old trick of turning every contingency into a resource for accumulating force in the Government.

"Albert J. Nock, in his great book entitled *Our Enemy—The State*, writes:

> Taking the State wherever found, striking into its history at any point, one sees no way to differentiate the activities of its founders, administrators and beneficiaries, from those of a professional, criminal class.

"While I could not give my wholehearted endorsement to such a statement, nevertheless there are innumerable cases where estates recovered, after corporation, income and inheritance taxes, less than 2/3 of a cent out of every dollar that the corporation originally earned. I leave it to you to decide —is that legitimate taxation, or has it become legalized thievery?"

If language denotes the thoughts and feelings of a man, the strong words of J. Howard Pew condemning confiscatory taxation revealed his great apprehension. To him, taxation that aims at government redistribution of wealth and income was objectionable on economic and moral grounds. He never tired of saying so publicly. And he never hesitated to condemn with harsh words the worst form of legalized thievery: inflation. During his long life he witnessed the gradual debauching of the U.S. dollar with its disastrous economic, social and political consequences. The proud American dollar which in his youth constituted approximately one-twentieth of an ounce of gold was reduced by 40 per cent in 1934, turned into a paper dollar first domestically, then internationally, and depreciated at ever faster rates until, at the time of his death, it was worth less than 25 cents of the gold dollar.

Long before the dollar inflation accelerated to two-digit rates J. Howard Pew warned us about the consequences of such a policy. In a speech to the Directors of the National Retail Dry Goods Association on January 10, 1949, he spoke as a wise and patient teacher.

"Inflation and price control, as cause and effect respectively, have been responsible for most of the tragedy and suffering inflicted upon humanity since the end of the barter era.

"Inflation is no new phenomenon. Most all of the nations of the world have suffered from it—many of them two or three times. But always it has either destroyed or left these nations in a seriously weakened condition.

"Wars, pestilences, plagues and catastrophes rarely bring

about the fall of a nation; but inflation has been responsible for the downfall of many great empires of the past.

"Those nations which have been afflicted with the scourge of inflation have suffered from a sequence of events which in every case seem to follow a definite pattern. Typical of this pattern is the fall of the Roman Empire.

"The Roman emperors, being desirous of providing more things for more people, so that they might be popular in the eyes of the public, and not wishing to alienate the goodwill of their people by imposing heavy taxes, resorted to the device of stamping out more coins; and then they used these coins to provide the people with circuses, all kinds of gratuities, and public works. For a time the scheme worked beautifully until finally the merchants discovered how the money of the realm was being debauched and demanded more of this money for their goods. At that time Diocletian was the emperor, and was furious that anyone should dare to question the integrity of his money. So he slapped on price controls. The merchants, who tried to sell at these prices, soon found themselves out of business because they could not sell real goods and accept therefor a debauched currency. And so the black markets sprang up all over the realm. Rationing was then imposed, followed by a control of wages, and the workers were told how, when and where they should work. Finally, there were so many rules and regulations, controls and mandates, imposed on the Roman people that they were no longer free to exercise their ingenuity and resourcefulness, and so they became frustrated. Life to them was no longer worth the living. They gradually resorted to all kinds of physical excesses and became dissolute, and the empire fell.

"Popular histories fail to give us these details. They tell us all about the exploits of the warriors and the politicians, but the economic conditions which implemented most of the important events in history are usually entirely overlooked. But most of this information is available, and I am having several groups working in the old libraries and gradually getting together much data on this subject.

"The pattern of the sequence of events which I have just cited as applying to Rome, can also be laid down as the cause of the fall of the Spanish Empire, the Byzantine Empire, Egypt, probably Greece, twice in France in the 16th and 18th centuries, and in a number of cases in the 20th century, with which you are already familiar.

"Now, what is inflation: Inflation is the increase in the quantity of money. There is some slight difference of opinion between economists as to this definition. While they all admit that inflation could not occur unless there had been an increase in the quantity of money, some hold that the actual inflation does not take place until that money is used or turned over. But I have failed to find any case in history where, once the money was created, it wasn't spent, and when it is spent it is used, and when it is used it turns over.

"How is this new money created? In the early days before the printing press, the government simply stamped out more coins. They usually kept the operations secret so that the people didn't at once discover what was going on. Later the government started the printing presses and flooded their countries with fiat money. Finally the process became more complex and confused but the results were substantially the same.

"Our Government caused the present inflation by selling their bonds to the banks. The banks then placed a credit to the Government for the amount of the bonds, and when the Government used this credit to pay their bills it created just that much new money—somewhere in the neighborhood of 80 billions of dollars. The magnitude of this increase in the quantity of money can best be visualized by comparing it with our national wealth in 1938, which has been estimated at 300 billions of dollars. If the Government can issue 80 billions of dollars of new money without causing a rise in prices or injuring our economy in any other way, why should they not issue 200 or even 1,000 billions of dollars? Why not have the Government finance all their expenses by printing-press money and stop taxing the people? The answer is, of course, that you can't get something for nothing—and this applies to governments just as much as it does to people.

"In the long run, inflation hurts everyone and helps nobody. It creeps into your safe deposit box and robs it of a part of everything there—and it does it without your knowledge and without even opening the box. It reaches into your pocket and steals a part of your money, without changing the numerals on the bills or the figures on the coins. It robs you of a part of the value of all your insurance policies, bank deposits, bonds, stock and government securities. Inflation is surely the greatest criminal of all time.

"Many people wonder how inflation has hurt industry. I have just completed a comprehensive study on the subject, and I found that the total cost of all plant and equipment now in use was 180 billions of dollars; and to replace this plant and equipment will cost 322 billions of dollars. The inflation, therefore, has cost industry 142 billions of dollars. According to my calculations, the total depreciation that was charged off for the year 1947 was approximately 9 billions of dollars, whereas the cost of replacing only that plant and equipment which has become worn out and obsolete will be between 16 and 18 billions of dollars. These figures show that there should be deducted from industry's 1947 earnings 7 billions of dollars or more for the replacement of plant and equipment worn out or become obsolete, 5 billions of dollars for inventory adjustments, or a total of 12 billions of dollars from the earnings of approximately 17 billions of dollars—which leaves the real 1947 earnings of industry five billions of dollars. This compares with the average earnings of industry over a 20-year period of 5 billions of dollars—but the 5 billions of real earnings in 1947 were in dollars which had only about half the purchasing power of the average earnings over the 20-year period.

"Now, what can the Government do about this whole question of inflation? Some people think that they should raise the interest rate on the government bonds so that they would be attractive to the people to purchase, and then compel the banks to sell all of their bonds to the people. While a small amount of this kind of thing might be beneficial to our economy, if carried on on a large scale it would bring about a deflation, which would undoubtedly cause a serious depresssion.

"It is my judgment that we should let bygones be bygones. The best economists of this country now are of the opinion that the inflation is gradually running its course and that it will stabilize itself in the not too distant future. We should bear in mind that industry has done a magnificent job during these last 9 years, for the volume of production is now 75 per cent higher than it was in 1939. There is little doubt but that the inflation can and will be stopped in the not too distant future—if the Government refrains from selling any additional bonds to the banks.

"Now, you say that this may all be true, but what has inflation to do with price control? Just this: The politicians have gone from one end of this country to the other, telling the people that high prices are the cause of inflation, and that the only way to stop inflation is to control prices. Of course, they have gotten the cart before the horse. High prices are no more the cause of inflation than wet streets are the cause of rain. High prices are the result of inflation, just as wet streets are the result of rain.

"The meanest criminal in the world is he who fixes the guilt for his crime on an innocent party. That is exactly what the politicians have done when they fix the guilt for inflation on business and industry."

J. Howard Pew reflected the monetary thought of the remnant of economists who in vain opposed the new economics of the Institutionalists and Keynesians. He was familiar with the writings of eminent economists, such as Frank A. Fetter, E. W. Kemmerer, B. M. Anderson, Friedrich A. Hayek, Henry Hazlitt, and Ludwig von Mises, and liked to refer to them in his public speeches. With Hazlitt and others of like mind he served on the Board of the Foundation for Economic Education, organized by Leonard Read to serve the free-enterprise remnant. But in spite of his close association and friendship with these kindred souls, J. Howard Pew remained an independent thinker who did not hesitate to voice his dissent. In the realm of inflation Pew probably made an original contribution to the body of monetary thought with his analysis of the effects of inflation on business profits and taxes. He recognized before anyone else that inflation leads to deceptive dollar profits and underdepreciation, which permits businessmen to live in a fool's paradise and government to extract additional levies from business. The following calculations by him cover the years 1947 and 1948; but they are even more pertinent today with two-digit rates of inflation. They help to explain the "energy crisis" which is characterized by huge dollar profits, exorbitant taxes and empty oil and gas tanks. In a speech to the American Petroleum Institute, on November 9, 1949, he described the forces of the coming energy crisis:

"Dollar profits during the years 1947 and 1948 have been high when compared with former years. But such a comparison is deceptive, for those were years of severe inflation which distorted completely the dollar yardstick. Let me illustrate what I mean:

"Oil men think in terms of oil—that is, property—not in terms of dollars. But, as corporate profits are calculated in dollars and not in property, inflation, because it reduces the purchasing power of money, raises the dollar value of property. When this property is sold, (and all industrial property except real estate is eventually marketed in the form of goods), a distortion in profits takes place and tends to make them appear far larger than they actually are.

"For two years, I have given considerable study to the magnitude of this distortion as applied to all industry. Time permits me only to highlight my findings. I shall be pleased to furnish anyone here a memorandum substantiating the following figures.

"As you are well aware, the cost of replacing plant and equipment today is usually from two to three times its original cost. Yet depreciation can be based only on original cost.

"My figures indicate that in each of the years 1947 and 1948 American non-financial corporations fell $10.1 billions short of recovering the current dollar cost of making good the annual wear, wastage and obsolescence of their facilities. If to these figures representing underdepreciation there be added so-called profits reported as earnings on inventory valuation and amounting to $8.2 billions in the same period, there has been, for the last two years, an overstatement of real profits by these corporations amounting to $28.4 billions.

"Now, if to these $28.4 billions are added the $24.3 billions of taxes paid by non-financial corporations to the Federal Government during these two years, we have a total of $52.7 billions. The total so-called profits before taxes of this same industrial group were $62.1 billions. The real profits of all American non-financial industry, therefore, after correcting for this inflation, distortion, were the difference between these figures, or approximately $9.4 billions—an average of $4.7 billions per year. Compare this, if you will, with the average annual industrial profits for this same group of $5.4 billions during the five prewar years.

"It is worthy of note, in passing, that on the basis of this realistic valuation of earnings American non-financial industry overpaid its Federal income taxes during these two years by $11.1 billions.

"Now, I ask you to compare these $9.4 billions of earnings

in the two years of our country's greatest peacetime production with the $38 billions of illusory and lush profits which the government, labor unions, and statistical organizations would have us believe were obtained.

"The seriousness of the problem grows out of the fact that unless industry can effect, as a result of its operations, the means with which to reproduce itself, as and when its plant and equipment are worn out, our great industrial machine will gradually shrivel up and die. For an appreciation of the misery and suffering that would follow such a disaster, look at Great Britain today!

"Let us tell this story to the American people, for millions of jobs depend on its proper solution. Labor leaders, socialists, and the enemies of American well-being are now using stories of legendary corporate profits to poison the minds of our people, so as to justify higher taxes, higher wages, and lower prices. It is vital that we take away from them this ammunition by telling the American people the unvarnished truth that these so-called profits simply do not exist, although some who prefer to live in a fool's paradise may find this task unpleasant."

Five

The Petroleum Industry, A Living Monument to the Enterprise System

"The whole history of the petroleum industry has been marked by unstinted competition—the kind of competition that always looks for better methods, improved processes, invention, discovery—the kind of competition that provides the consumer with constantly improved products at lower costs."*

J. HOWARD PEW was an oil man. He was born in a family that was engaged in gas and oil exploration, and spent his long productive life in the development of his family business. For sixty-nine years he examined and analyzed oil, tested and researched it, explored the uses to which it could be put, investigated its markets, managed its production and directed the creative efforts of many thousands of men. Indeed, few men, if any, have contributed so much to the growth of the modern petroleum industry as did J. Howard Pew. Due to his labors and those of other great entrepreneurs the modern petroleum industry, which dates back to Drake's Titusville well of 1859, underwent a most significant change. In its first half-century when the industry was guided largely by John D. Rockefeller, petroleum products were used mainly as illuminants. During the next half-century many petroleum products were developed as sources of power and heat, which has made the in-

*J. Howard Pew Address before Empire State Petroleum Association, April 11, 1946.

120

dustry the most important producer of "energy," giving economic comfort and well-being to countless millions of people.

To J. Howard Pew this miracle of economic development sprang from the liberation of human energy from the age-old bondage of statism. He never tired talking about the American enterprise system that gave birth to a new age of economic production and human well-being. In a speech to the National Society Magna Charta Dames, on November 15, 1955, he explained progress like this:

"For over a hundred years freedom flourished in our land. When I graduated from college in 1900, America truly was the land of opportunity. Had the government at that time been disposed to control our economic activities, as they are today, the oil industry to which I have devoted over 50 years of my life, might well have been an entirely different industry than that which it is today. Let me tell you something about the development of the oil industry and its companion, the motor car industry; and at the same time speculate with you as to what might have been the attitude of a national economic planning board back in the year 1900, if one had existed at that time, toward these industries.

"At that time there were being operated in this country some 8,500 motor cars, consuming approximately 85,000 barrels of gasoline a year. That is just about enough gasoline to keep the cars of today on the road for two minutes. Now let us imagine Mr. Ford, with his great vision of the automobile's future, appearing before that board and asking that in their program for the next decade they provide a few billions of dollars of capital along with the necessary labor and material, for his industry. The board would have recognized in Mr. Ford a mild lunatic. They would have asked him where he expected to get the gasoline for all those cars; and would have pointed out that neither the gasoline nor the crude oil from which to make it was anywhere in sight—and they would have refused Mr. Ford's request. A sophisticated public would have laughed at Mr. Ford when the board set down genius as insanity and inventive ability as lunacy; and that would have ended all foolish talk about horseless carriages and flying machines.

"But fortunately for the 40 millions of families in this country who today derive pleasure and satisfaction from the operation of their cars, there was no such board in the year 1900. And so Mr. Ford, not worrying about where his gasoline was coming from, went right ahead building more cars and better cars, until presently he was turning out over a million cars a year.

"Fortunately, too, for the petroleum industry that there was no such board, for oil men, too, went right ahead drilling more wells and deeper wells and sometimes finding oil. They brought technology to their assistance in the form of geology and geophysics, and by their aid discovered new oil fields. And so the oil industry, doing each year those things which would have been impossible the year before, was always able to keep just a step ahead of the thirst for gasoline of those multiplying millions of automobiles.

"I heard a little more about the developments of Ford's business the other day, which I checked up myself before I could believe it. Ford started with a small capital of $28,000. The first year he turned out 1,708 cars. At the end of 20 years his enterprise was turning out over 2,000,000 cars per year. That happened because Ford plowed 68 per cent of his earnings back into his business. Today that cannot be done. The taxers and the equalizers do not permit it.

"There were no corporation income taxes in Ford's day. Today corporations pay 50 per cent of their income in taxes. If the equalizers and the taxers in Ford's day had reduced the amount which he could plow back by one-half, the growth of his business would have been reduced, not by a half, but by 98 per cent. At the end of 20 years, under such conditions Mr. Ford would have been able to produce, not 2,000,000 cars per year, but only 40,000 cars. Had that happened, Mr. Ford would not have been the loser. His profit from the production of 40,000 cars would have been more than sufficient for his needs and even his desires. The loser would have been the American people. They would have lost the jobs and the opportunities created by his great enterprise. They would have been denied the benefits of a rise in living standards that comes from capital funds put back into productive work. Attempts to equalize wealth is the way to destroy it. But most of us are prone to harbor just a little resentment toward those who possess more than we do. This can be illustrated by a little story.

"Pat and Mike were great personal friends. One evening when they waxed confidential, Pat said to Mike:

Mike, if you owned a house and I didn't, you would let me sleep in one of your rooms, wouldn't you?
Sure and I would.
And if you owned a horse and I didn't, you would let me drive him, wouldn't you?
Sure and I would.
And if you owned a cow and I didn't, you would share the milk with me, wouldn't you?
Sure and I would.
And if you owned a pig and I didn't and you butchered it, you would share the meat with me, wouldn't you?
No, begorra, I got a pig!

"The first telephone was installed on the White House desk of General Grant. After he had talked into his end of the wire and listened to the answering voice coming in from the other end, until he was thoroughly satisfied that the thing really would work, he leaned back in his chair and said: 'Yes, it is truly remarkable; but who in the world would ever want to use one of them?' Now, General Grant was quite a man. He won a great war and was twice President. But I submit that that incident justifies the gravest doubts about the wisdom of any economic planning board which he might have appointed

—and as President, according to our present-day planners, he would have had to appoint just such a board.

"Now, some people think that we do not have such boards today; but let me call your attention to a few—such as, the Federal Trade Commission, Federal Power Commission, Securities and Exchange Commission, the Interstate Commerce Commission. Sometime ago I received a letter from the research director of the Commission on Organization, in which he said that there are at least 50 boards, commissions, and so on which deal directly with economic affairs; and then stated that the Federal agencies having economic implications are legion. The existence of every one of these organizations violates, as I shall later point out, the intent and purpose of the Constitution and the Bill of Rights, if not their very wording.

"Let me tell you just one more story which I ran across in a report put out by the Patent Office Society, and which I consider to be the richest one of them all. About the middle of the last century, it was proposed in Washington to build a new building to house the Patent Office. The Congressional Committee called in Mr. Ellsworth, who was then United States Commissioner of Patents, to ask his advice. Commissioner Ellsworth counseled against too large or expensive a building, because invention had just about reached its limit. He related the astounding advances that had been made in the mechanical arts during his lifetime, and predicted a cessation of activity in the field of invention—there just wasn't anything else left to invent.

"At this point I made a little investigation of my own, and I found that up until Ellsworth's time there had been taken out in this country some 3,327 patents; but that since then almost three million patents have been granted—just a little increase of some 90,000 per cent. So much for that one government official who undoubtedly would have been a member of the national economic planning board, if one had existed at that time. But Commissioner Ellsworth was not so illiberal as are most of our present-day planners. He didn't believe there could be many more inventions, but in any event he did not propose to suppress them when they did come along."

During the early 1930's the American railroads launched a powerful political campaign aiming to impose severe restrictions and heavy taxes on commercial use of the highways. Hurt by the Great Depression, they could think of no other solution to their problems than to suppress the competition by the trucking industry. In all the state legislatures the railroad lobby introduced legislative measures that would have forced commercial vehicles off the road.

To J. Howard Pew this legislative drive by the railroad lobby was a flagrant attempt at establishing a monopoly. He rose in defense of competition and helped to defeat the restriction schemes. At a mass rally in Philadelphia, on April 12, 1933, he refuted the lobby arguments through a masterly use of analogy:

"Our state faces the question of what uses its highways are to serve, and who is to pay for them. The railroads demand taxes and 'regulation' to drive commercial traffic off the highways, in order that they may force that traffic back to the rails.

"Now, I am in the oil business, and if the legislature would drive everybody else out of the oil business and leave it all to my Company, it would make things a lot easier for me. And if the legislature does that much for the railroads, I see no reason why it should not for me.

"Next to having all the oil business legislated over to our Company, I should like to have minimum prices fixed for our competitors. Just let us name our own prices for gasoline, and keep those of our competitors a few cents higher, and we'll try to wriggle through the depression somehow. That's another thing the railroads are demanding at Harrisburg this winter, and if they get it I don't see why I should not.

"The railroads' propaganda this winter has given me a lot of good ideas for helping business. It is a pet theory of the railroads that more taxes—that is, more taxes paid by the other fellow—would be the ideal business restorer.

"A man who manufactures shoes told me the other day that he was convinced that trucks ought to pay more than they do; he thought gasoline taxes and license taxes ought to be raised, because that would get more money to build more roads; and the folks who used them would pay for them. I said it was a good scheme, and called his attention to the fact that a bill had been introduced at Harrisburg to require 3-foot sidewalks alongside all state highways.

"'Now,' I said, 'there is a bill you shoe manufacturers ought to support. Build sidewalks along all highways and people will walk more, thus wearing out more shoes. Then put a 100 per cent tax on the manufacturer's cost of every pair of shoes, and provide that this shoe tax be used to pay for the sidewalks. That's how gasoline taxes pay for the roads. A national shoe tax would produce about $750,000,000 annually; the manufacturer would pass it on to the consumer, so it wouldn't hurt the industry. In fact it would be a good thing, because with all those sidewalks people would walk so much, and wear out so many shoes, that the shoe industry would be securely back on its feet in no time at all.'

"My shoe manufacturing friend didn't seem enthusiastic about my plan. In fact I find that nobody seems enthusiastic about increasing his own taxes, so they have all concentrated on boosting automotive and oil taxes. The railroads, since they discovered how to get more money from the Reconstruction Finance Corporation than they pay out in taxes, have been particularly strong for taxing the other fellow. . . .

"In many states this season, the railroads have pressed bills to authorize public authority to fix minimum rates for truck service. Of course that means that the minimum rate would be fixed with reference to the railroad rates; that is, the lowest truck rate would presumably be set high enough to give the railroads a good chance at the business. Unless they hope for at least that much, the railroads would have no reason to ask such a law; and they are asking it very generally. Now, it is plainly impossible to fix the price of one service or commodity with reference to another. Can you imagine a law to fix prices of bread with a view to insuring that it shouldn't supplant beef in the market? Or is it conceivable that a commission should fix the price of potatoes with a view to insuring a market for rice? Or that the rates for electric light should be determined, not with the aim of reasonableness, but with the purpose of giving gas a share in the market? All these analogies strike us as foolish; yet they show just what is in the minds of people who want minimum truck rates fixed by commissions. Nobody except the railroads ever asked to have minimum rates fixed for truck service—and the railroads couldn't possibly have but one purpose. That is, to insure them some business, at higher rates, that they couldn't get at lower rates.

"The point is that the truck and the railroad don't render the same service. You can't fix the rate for one in terms of the other. Can you imagine a law saying that a bushel of wheat should always sell for the same as a bushel-and-a-half of potatoes? It would be just as reasonable: wheat and potatoes are both foods: railroads and trucks are both transportation agencies. But when a man's appetite demands a potato it isn't going to be satisfied with a slice of bread; and when his business requires the special facilities the truck affords he isn't going to use the railroad, if he can help it. The truck renders what may be called a personal service; the railroad, a highly impersonal one. The truck does the particular thing you want done just as and when you order it. It follows your order clear through, store-door to store-door; the railroads can't do that, and don't do it."

Several years later when the Allied Powers made prepara-

tions for a peaceful world after the human tragedy that was
World War II, the U.S. Government set out to restrict competition through international agreements. And again, J.
Howard Pew through speeches, articles and testimonies
before Congressional committees rose to defend competition.

"How alluring are those words: Stability! Order! Cooperation! Planned Economy! But out of the bitter experience
of the last few years we have learned that such words were
the sheep's clothing under which the wolf of National Socialism hid. We have learned that such specious phrases point
toward governmental controls that crushed the freedom of individuals and point toward an economic collectivism which
is the antithesis of the American competitive enterprise system.

"Many of these men for the last twelve years have been
seeking to force a system of collectivism upon us with only
partial success. Now they see the opportunity of establishing
such a system in this country through the rear door of international treaties and agreements. In this way, they apparently hope to achieve in a constitutional manner what otherwise
would be unconstitutional. The Constitution makes treaties
the supreme law of the land, on a par with the Constitution
itself, overriding other Federal laws, and State constitutions
and laws which may be in conflict with the treaty. In this period when our Government is in the process of negotiating a
multitude of treaties and international agreements, we should
be very alert to the possibility that through such activities
the entire political and economic structure of this country
may be radically changed.

"As a matter of fact an attempt already has been made in
this direction. Last August our Government suddenly promul-
gated a proposed Anglo-American Oil Agreement. Under the
guise of assuring equal opportunity for the Nationals of these
two countries to develop oil resources in their respective jur-
isdictions, this Agreement provided a framework for restrictions on the production of petroleum and its products, the

fixing of prices and the allocation of marketing quotas upon the recommendations of an International Petroleum Commission. Inherent in the implications of the Agreement was the assumption of an obligation by our Federal Government, when it concurred in such recommendations, to undertake to carry them out in the domestic field. Now the fulfillment of such an obligation would necessitate the exercise by the Federal Government of an authority which it does not now possess under our Constitution, because jurisdiction over natural resources is among the powers reserved to the States in the Tenth Amendment.

"But once a treaty such as the Anglo-American Oil Agreement were concluded, our Federal Government would attain the authority through the treaty-making powers to assume virtually an absolute authority over the production and distribution of petroleum and its products in this country.

"The Anglo-American Petroleum Agreement as it was submitted to the Senate last fall constituted nothing short of a super-state cartel. Such cartelization would constitute national socialization of the petroleum industry here and abroad. Fortunately the unanimous protest of the American petroleum industry succeeded in blocking the effectuation of the scheme, at least for the time being.

"Throughout the controversy over the Oil Agreement, it was difficult to avoid the conclusion that those who had proposed it were desirous of taking a shortcut designed to change our American system overnight to the status of the German system of National Socialism. If you regard that as a fanciful thought, just remember that the advocates of Socialism long have proposed the promotion of cartels in the conviction that a system of extensive monopolies controlled by the State paved the way for a socialist economy. Hitler and Mussolini never could have risen to positions of absolute control had they not had a ready-made system of cartels to work on.

"Much of what I have said specifically in regard to the Oil

Treaty is applicable to similar undertakings affecting other industries. This use of the treaty-making power to override constitutional limitations and set the stage for transforming our American system into National Socialism is a danger that may engulf all of us. During the controversy over the Petroleum Agreement, it was reported that similar international agreements were contemplated covering approximately 60 commodities and services in international trade. These were said to cover grain, rubber, tin, sugar, coffee, shipping cargo space and global airways. Undoubtedly, others had to do with metals, leather, wool, cotton, chemicals, as well as manufactured articles that could be fitted into a cartel framework. All would be knit together into an integrated whole under the direction of an International Trade Authority.

"Those plans are sufficiently broad, if pursued, to encompass a large part of world trade in a super-state cartel system. More alarming, however, this movement would entangle a large part of our domestic economy in the tentacles of the vicious cartel system, with destructive repercussions upon every other line of economic activity.

"The amazing thing is that this scheme for super-state cartels has won the support of men who agree that the private cartel is evil and reprehensible. Yet they profess to believe that an undertaking that is against the public welfare and thus bad, can be made good if it is conducted under the aegis of government." (From an address to the Toledo Rotary Club, June 25, 1945).

In an article written for the *National Petroleum News* (August 19, 1946) Mr. Pew brilliantly refuted the only argument that is ever raised on behalf of international control. His answer is as cogent and irrefutable today in the decade of the "energy crisis" as it was in 1946 when the allied governments endeavored to manage the world.

"In fact, only one justification has been advanced in behalf of embroiling our domestic industry in a network of international control. It is that we are running out of oil in America. It is a phony argument. It has been made for years—at the time of World War I; after that conflict; in the late twenties; again in the middle thirties; during the last war, and still we hear it. It always has been the same; we shall run out of oil within 14 to 20 years 'if' something or other does not happen. This always has been *"iffy"* speculation and scare talk.

"Of course, 'if' we do not discover any more oil, we shall run out of it. Of course, 'if' the sun fails to come up tomorrow, we shall be in a devil of a fix. But the sun will come up and only simpletons would spend their time figuring what they would do, 'if' it did not come up. So, too, we discover more oil every day and shall continue to do so as long as Americans remain free men and our competitive enterprise system provides incentives for them to put forth the necessary effort."

His great faith in the productive energy of free men led J. Howard Pew to reject all government attempts at price fixing of petroleum products. During the early thirties he liked to cite the writings of such eminent economists as Sumner H. Slichter, George E. Roberts, G. F. Warren, Simon Litman, Frank A. Fetter, Chester H. Gray, and Robert F. Martin, all of whom raised cogent objections against various price fixing schemes. As a respected spokesman of the petroleum industry J. Howard Pew applied general economic knowledge to the intricacies and specialties of his industry. Above all, he demonstrated convincingly how government controls over some petroleum prices would lead to comprehensive price controls over all prices and thus destroy the intricate working of the market system. In particular, he showed how government control over transportation prices, which are important petroleum industry costs, would be very harmful to the whole energy industry. In an essay written in 1934, entitled "Price Fixing for Petroleum Products," with examples and figures taken from the early 1930's, J. Howard Pew already described the energy crisis of the 1970's.

"It will be worthwhile to consider the effects of price fixing in petroleum, as was recently proposed in an elaborate scheme put out by the Planning and Coordinating Committee for the industry. First, the industry would have to be brought under complete Government domination, from the wildcatter to the filling-station retailer. But in petroleum this would be vastly more difficult than in any other product, for an effective control of all petroleum operations necessarily presumes the cooperation of Federal and State Governments and of the endless interests and competing factors within the industry. The market for petroleum and its products is as wide as the continent; but most petroleum production comes from a few states. In all of these it is among the most valued sources of private wealth and public revenue. These states naturally are jealous to insure for their people, and for their public treasuries, the largest possible benefits and advantages. The extent to which Federal authority may interfere with this regional interest is by no means certain. There are legal and constitutional questions that have not been wholly answered.

"Further, because of the endless complexities of this industry, price fixing presumes complete government control. If we should have price fixing for crude, with prices of products fixed, there must be control and regulation of every intermediate process. The Government must determine where and how often wells may be drilled, and must fix the price of oil when produced; must determine how much of it may be produced by each state, by each oil field within the state, and ultimately by each well.

"Such close control necessarily presumes also a like control of transportation, distribution to refineries, and allocation of areas to be served by particular dealers. Transportation is one of the largest items in manufacturing cost of gasoline. The balance of the consumer's price is made up of first cost to the wholesaler, taxes, marketing expense, overhead, allowance to the retailer, and capital charges. But transportation is so great a factor that it must be brought under control. But here, again, there is competition to be dealt with. A few years ago gasoline was transported by rail in tank cars—practically all of it. More recently, pipelines have been used to transport gasoline, so that today great pipeline systems bring both oil and gasoline from the southwestern oil fields into the upper Mississippi and Great Lakes areas at less than half the cost of rail transportation. The Great Lakes Pipe Line Company has a gasoline line from the Oklahoma field almost due north through Kansas, Missouri and Iowa to Des Moines where it forks, one branch going to St. Paul, another to Chicago and Milwaukee and a third to Omaha. The Phillips Pipe Line runs from Borger, Texas, to East St. Louis. These two lines carry about 48,000 barrels of gasoline daily out of Oklahoma and Texas for the grain belt states. To fix the price of gasoline throughout all these states, on the basis of rail rates, would be to deny the public the benefits of the cheaper pipeline transportation. Yet that was proposed in the schedule offered by the Planning and Coordinating Committee.

"But that is not all. Other pipelines bring crude oil to a great number of refineries in the Corn Belt states, where refineries turn it into gasoline and kerosene at prices far below cost based on *rail* transportation from the oil country. To base gasoline prices in this region on full rail transportation costs, would be as archaic as to charge for pig iron at Pittsburgh on the basis of costs at Bethlehem plus freighting across Pennsylvania by Conestoga wagon. Transportation by lake and river extensively supplements these pipeline systems, at an enormous saving; but all this economy would be wiped out by the simple device of basing the consumer's price on full rail rates.

"In fixing its Pacific Coast prices, the Planning and Coordinating Committee again distorted the relationship of transportation to price. California produces more crude and more products than the coast area can use. It ships large quantities of both crude and products to the eastern seaboard. Despite this the Planning and Coordinating Committee schedule fixes the Pacific Coast price basis one cent above the Gulf Coast price—as if to cover transportation costs from the Gulf. That is just about as logical as it would be to fix the price of flour in Minnesota on the basis of the Minneapolis cost plus freight from New York. 'Carrying coals to Newcastle' has become a proverbial description of wasteful transportation. But the Planning and Coordinating Committee goes farther; it demands that Newcastle pay for that transportation, even though it never takes place!

"The price structure of the entire business is dependent upon transportation costs. Changes in transportation rates and methods could easily disrupt the entire price fabric, rearrange distribution areas, and wreck all relationships within the industry. Now this industry has always been largely one of transportation. Pipelines date back to the earliest years of the old Pennsylvania oil fields. Since that time the industry has developed a transportation system adapted to its peculiar circumstances and purposes, by far the cheapest and most efficient in the world. But for this unique transportation organization, the industry as we know it simply could not have come into being. It gave our country those supplies of cheap motor fuel that made possible our 25,000,000 motor cars, our automotive industry, our modern highways. This transportation system includes over 106,000 miles of crude oil lines, and 3,800 miles of gasoline lines. It includes 549 ocean tank ships; over 100,000 railroad tank cars, and about 150,000 tank trucks. Over 25 per cent of all railroad revenues from manufactures comes from petroleum products alone! Over 25 per cent of Panama Canal tolls comes from petroleum and its products. The oil tanker fleet represents 24.4 per cent of all ocean-going tonnage under the American flag.

"The whole industry, from the search for oil in the ground to the workings of the curb-side gasoline pump, is completely bound up with the problems, facilities and costs of transportation. The most casual change in freight rates could cut a refiner off from his sources of crude, or divorce him from his distributing territory. So, to fix prices means that this whole complex of transportation rates must also be fixed and the fixing of transportation rates in one great industry must compel a like control of rates in other industries.

"The oil industry falls into four grand divisions: Producing, Refining, Transportation and Marketing. Some units are engaged exclusively in one division, some in two or three, and some in all four. One man produces oil; another pipes it to the Gulf Coast; still another transports it by tanker to a refinery on the North Atlantic Coast; the refiner sells its products to jobbers, who sell them to wholesalers, who pass them on to retailers. Again they are transported by tanker, barge, pipeline, railroad and truck before they can acutally go through the retailer's pump, to the consumer. In this long series of operations, each must be paid for out of the final selling price. Whenever Government fixes prices for crude at one end and products at the other, all intermediate steps must be brought into line. The rates of all transporters and handlers must be under Government domination—checked, policed and controlled. Not only the runs of crude at each refinery, but the amount of gasoline it may turn out, the quantity it may sell, where and to whom it may be sold—all this must be controlled. Nowhere would there be left any initiative for the individual.

"A governmental administration capable of thus controlling such a business structure would be impossible. Any governmental agency clothed with such enormous authority and discretion could not possibly avoid accusations of partiality. It would live in an atmosphere surcharged with suspicion and hostility. It would have to check the production of 320,000 wells bringing forth from a fraction of a barrel to several thousand barrels daily per well. It would have to keep tabs on the runs of crude in some 540 refineries, and on their daily output. It must be sure that total products balanced the allowance of crude, and that amounts of products distributed balances with both of these. It would have to keep in touch with all transportation, and to watch some 350,000 retailers operating 1,000,000 gasoline pumps. There are 25,000,000 motor vehicles, making from 2,500,000,000 to 3,000,000,000 retail purchases a year. These must be watched and kept in balance with the prescribed prices and permitted quantities. To set up such a machinery of policing and administration would be impossible."

J. Howard Pew was convinced that the very existence of the American oil industry depends on individual freedom, which is the freedom to compete, work and invest, to strive for material improvement. Freedom is the absence of government coercion and political power that check the prosperity of the people and weaken their energy, intellect and virtues. A free economy presumes the freedom to compete in a setting of equality before the law.

But unfortunately, the government of the United States no longer honors our equal right to liberty, property and protection of the laws. Since the 1930's it has bestowed important legal immunities and privileges to certain pressure groups that evidence political power. In the words of J. Howard Pew:

"A free economy is only possible when all people stand equal before the law. That is the principle laid down in our Constitution. That is the principle that has made America great. That is primarily the principle that has enabled our American workers to produce three times as much goods as have the workers in Europe.

"But this principle has been violated time after time in the last few years; for the Administration has—either for political reasons or prejudice, or both—given scandalous preference to the CIO. The Wagner Act was bad enough, but the New Deal courts have interpreted it to be far worse than was intended. They have given organized labor immunity from monopoly, anti-trust laws, extortion, riots; and even have protected them when they mass picketed a plant and stopped its production when no labor dispute or disturbance of any kind existed. In Boston a man and his wife owned a restaurant. They employed no outside help. And because they sold their food a little cheaper than some of the competing restaurants, their place was picketed by CIO workers, they were able to get no protection from the lawless elements, and were driven out of business—and the highest Court in our land sustained the right of the CIO to do such picketing. As the law stands today, the United States Supreme Court have certainly held that anarchy is now a Constitutional activity within our borders. Unless a law be enacted within the not too distant future, in which the labor unions, with all other segments of our people, are to be adjudged equally before the law—then it will be the end of our free system of competitive enterprise." (From an address to Retired Bank Officers Association, Nov. 30, 1945.)

Occasionally CIO spokesmen made irresponsible attacks on Mr. Pew and members of his family. Steeped in Marxian economics, they would charge the Pew family with "labor exploitation" and "monopolistic practices." When, in an election campaign, some officials made such charges over the American Broadcasting System, J. Howard Pew received equal time for his answer:

"As to the charge—which I resent most of all—that I desire 'to exploit labor' and destroy competition by monopolistic means, my actions speak louder than any words of mine could.

"The American petroleum industry, according to the Bureau of Labor Statistics, is and always has been one of the highest wage industries in the country. Today it tops the list. Sun Oil Company always has paid wages and provided employee benefits as high or higher than oil companies with which we compete. We are known far and wide as *a high wage Company.* Our employees do not think they are being exploited. In the sixty years my family has been in the oil business those activities have never been marked by a single strike.

"The confidence and faith of Sun Oil employees in their Company is further evidenced by the fact that 7,000 of 12,000 employees engaged in oil activities own Company stock, under a plan set up twenty years ago to give them an opportunity to become owners as well as workers.

"It always has been our belief and practice that no business is truly successful unless its success means something substantial for its workers.

"Sun Oil's subsidiary, Sun Shipbuilding and Drydock Company, likewise is rated as paying the highest wages and producing the lowest cost ships in that industry—which also pays top wages among the durable goods industries. The few labor disputes that have occurred over the years in that enterprise have been quickly adjusted.

"As for the untruthful charge of engaging in monopolistic practices to destroy competitors, we have fought unceasingly, by word and by deed, every proposal involving restraint of trade from N.R.A. codes, to international cartels, to price controls. We believe in competition for ourselves. We have never sought special privilege nor a sheltered position.

"Our attitude always has been we have no divine right to a place and share in our industry. If somebody else can serve the public better in quality or price, he is entitled to the business.

"In order to keep the picture in proper perspective it should be noted that Sun Oil is one of the smaller units of the petroleum industry, doing about four or five per cent of the country's petroleum business. Thus, as a small business unit, our sympathies and interest lie with the ambitions and aspirations of the small fellow for freedom of opportunity.

"Our philosophy always has been that business and industry render their greatest service to the Nation when they constantly produce better commodities and services at lower prices through an efficiency that reconciles a low cost policy with the payment of high wages.

"Such has been our practice, evidenced by constantly improved products, and the passing of the savings in lowered costs on to our customers in reduced prices and to our employees in higher wages.

"Surely these facts, which I challenge anyone to dispute, expose the falsity of charges of labor exploitation and monopolistic practices. Indeed, to any fair-minded person they demonstrate the very opposite." (From his remarks over ABC, on June 22, 1946).

As the chief executive of a large oil company, Mr. Pew frequently faced the Marxian argument that big business tends to get bigger and bigger, swallowing small enterprises until it becomes a monopolistic monster that exploits its workers and gouges its consumers. Therefore, the U.S. Government must be called upon to save the weak competition of small enterprises through antitrust restraints and controls. Remembering the years when Sun Oil Company was merely a fledgling business in Pittsburgh and Toledo, J. Howard Pew simply rejected this popular argument as "foolish talk."

"We hear a lot of foolish talk about the way bigger business destroys smaller business. People seem to confuse the word 'bigger' with 'better.' Better business will succeed, whether it be large or small. We are apt to forget that big business was once small business, and the small business grew into big business because it had good management and freedom to grow. But freedom is the vital factor, because without freedom there can be no such thing as competition, and without competition there can be no such thing as good management." (Presentation of the Medal of Honor of the Hall of Free Enterprise to Leonard E. Starr on April 29, 1965).

In 35 years as chief executive of Sun Oil Company, J. Howard Pew guided a small company of oil men to grow to a world-wide enterprise in oil and gas exploration, refining, marketing and shipbuilding, with some 8,800 producing oil and gas wells, 17,100 service stations, 7 North American refineries and one in Liberia, Africa, 5,500 miles of crude oil gathering lines and trunk lines, 2,100 miles of product lines, 8 oceangoing tankers, with assets of $3 billion, giving employment to some 27,000 workers, utilizing the savings of more than 40,000 stockholders. Under his presidency Sun Oil Company grew more than twentyfold. What were the secrets of his great leadership and phenomenal success? He had a creed by which he worked and which guided him in countless business decisions. He trusted God for great things. God entrusted him with talent and wealth and showed him the way to lead thousands. In a speech to a Retired Bank Officers Association on November 30, 1945, he talked about his trusteeship:

"I like to think of the role that management plays in our modern business as a trusteeship—for management is entrusted with the interests of employees, investors and the consumers. If management fails to provide each group with that to which it is fairly entitled, then the interests of all three groups are jeopardized.

"I have always believed that the biggest job of management is that of sound human relations. This is not only true because the employees represent the largest number of contacts which must be made in any industrial establishment, but because there is almost no limit to the amount of goods that the workers can produce if they approach their jobs with the right spirit and good will. And so in the Sun Oil Company the top man in every department is held responsible first of all for his human relations. We give this man an assistant who is capable of handling the routine operations of the business. This top man brings all of the men together periodically and talks to them. The vice president in charge meets with all of them when occasion offers. And I make it a rule to contact most of the workers once a year, when I explain to them such things as: Production is the key to prosperity—the more goods that are produced, the greater will be our prosperity—workers, management and investors. I outline to them the principles which the Company believes in. I try to tell them some homely stories. I believe that the president of every industrial corporation ought to contact, in groups, every employee at least once a year and should talk to them. This will require a large percentage of his time, but if he can get even 10 per cent more production as a result of it, he is making the greatest possible contribution to his Company's success. The Company can well supply him with an executive vice president to look after routine operations."

In a speech to the Independent Refinery Workers Union, on July 28, 1944, J. Howard Pew spoke in greater detail about the "sound principles" that governed every action of his company.

"The first of these is sound *human relations*. This means that everyone in the Company is a human being and should be treated as such. Fairness and justice for all must be our motto. Each should be adequately rewarded for his or her services. Do you know that 97 per cent of all the new businesses which are started fail in a few years? The reason they fail is very largely because they do not have the proper human relations. Without proper human relations there does not exist the proper spirit and will to produce. It is only the companies that produce the most goods per worker that eventually succeed. The oil industry, like many others, is a highly competitive one; and if our Company is to live and prosper, we must all realize that production is the key to success.

"Then there is what I term our *trusteeship*. The Company is entrusted with the interests of its stockholders and with the human relations of its workers. It is also the trustee of the public, which holds the Company responsible for turning out good products at prices which are fair and equitable. The American people will permit its private corporations to operate only so long as they can make a good accounting of their stewardship.

"Next is *good will*. What our customers think of us. Good products, fairly priced, will go a long way to obtain their good will. But the public also wants to feel that we have established good human relations, and that we have made a good accounting of our stewardship.

"I consider that the maintenance and erection of adequate *buildings* and *plant* is a most important principle. I do not want to dwell at length on this. We do know that old and obsolete plant and equipment throws a financial burden on business which it cannot long support.

"The fifth principle has to do with *finance*. I believe that a company should never pay out so much money, either in dividends to its stockholders or in wages to its workers, as to weaken its capital structure. This is important to the stockholders; but it is of far greater importance to the workers, because it is the best insurance for them that they are going to have jobs.

"Now we come to *research*. I might have placed this at the head of the list, because that is what prevents a company from going to seed. I believe a corporation should always spend sufficient money on research to adequately develop new processes for making new and better products; then to build new plants to employ more men, with higher wages for all. This is the policy we have followed so successfully in the past. That is the policy which will insure us a great future.

"The last principle which I have in mind is *service*. There is an old story that if you build a better mouse trap than anybody else, the world will make a beaten path to your door. But that simply isn't true. Even though we observe carefully the six principles which I have already mentioned and neglect service, the Company will fail. There we have the whole picture.

"So we see that the answer as to what happens to us rests largely in our hands. If we are living in a political and economic atmosphere conducive to individual initiative, and if we exercise that initiative by increasing our efficiency and production—and I refer to every one of us—then the Sun Oil Company will be able to continue to pay higher and higher wages and to offer to the public better and better products at lower and lower prices. So long as we do that, we need not fear our future. A job with a company which pursues these policies is the best insurance which we can have against the vicissitudes of life.

"After all, happiness is our principal aim in life, and that is my greatest wish for you tonight. Neither the loafer nor the drunk is happy, because both have lost their self-respect. I have found that service and hard work are the first requisites of a happy life. The woman who struggles to raise her family—the man who works to produce something worthwhile in the world—receive that satisfaction which comes from a knowledge that they are contributing, to the greatest of his or her ability, to the welfare of their family, their State and their Country."

J. Howard Pew could have mentioned another principle of management that guided him in his important decisions. From time to time he would *challenge* his men to achieve the impossible. He would call on his company to embark upon difficult ventures of discovery and production. When Sun Oil Company undertook the development of Athabasca Tar Sands in Northern Alberta, a decade before the energy crisis and before other competitors dared to follow, he revealed to Sun Oil stockholders his motive for the costly venture: "Unless projects of this kind are periodically challenged and solved, our organization will become soft and eventually useless." At the dedication of the production plant, on September 30, 1967, Mr. Pew then proudly reported that the research and development department had succeeded in evolving a practical and economical method for producing a high quality synthetic crude oil from the Tar Sands. "The task of achieving this product has been a difficult and arduous one. Its accomplishment was due to the initiative, resourcefulness, ingenuity, inventiveness and hard work of literally hundreds of Sun's scientists, engineers and technicians." For a job well done Mr. Pew gave his men his highest praise: "My associates have conceived and built this magnificent plant. And so I trust that they now take comfort in the knowledge that they have not become soft and that they are most useful."

For many years of J. Howard Pew's company control, in hundreds of Sun Offices around the globe, the principles that guided him in his illustrious career were proudly displayed as the Company Creed. It is a simple document of the basic principles of a successful enterprise in the capitalist order at its best, a document that does lasting honor to the Company, its founders and its men, as well as to the order that made it all possible.

The Creed We Work By

A Statement of Principles

Recognizing that business exists to serve the common good and appreciating that our stewardship is properly of broad interest to many people, we of Sun Oil Company wish to set forth the principles which guide us in the conduct of our business affairs.

We believe in America as a land able under God to enrich its people, both materially and spiritually, even more abundantly in the future than it has in the past.

We believe our Company's principal role in America's future will be to develop petroleum and other energy resources, to process petroleum and related raw materials into high quality products for sale at competitive prices, and to provide such services as will help us to accomplish these ends most effectively.

We believe that the competitive system of free markets is the only effective regulator of economic enterprise, the only guarantor of efficient public service, and the indispensable protector not only of economic freedom but of all American freedom and opportunity.

We believe the opportunity to earn profits is the essential incentive to economic progress; that the ability to earn profits as a means of maintaining a sound financial structure, compensating stockholders for the use of their savings, and providing funds for growth to satisfy consumer demands, is the ultimate test of the real worth of a business to the people it serves.

We believe sound business and moral considerations dictate that we exercise integrity in all dealings with customers, employes, and stockholders, balancing the interests of each group so that all may share fairly, along with the general public, in the benefits to be derived from our business.

We believe in the right of employes to receive individual consideration and recognition, dignified treatment, and opportunity for self-improvement and advancement and, in addition, to negotiate collectively in their mutual interest.

We believe that stockholders, as the people who make our business possible through the investment of their savings, are entitled to a return at least equal to the return they might receive from other investments entailing similar risks.

We believe that the interests of customers, employes and stockholders alike dictate that we conduct all operations with the highest degree of efficiency, seeking constantly through training and the modernization of plants and equipment to reduce the cost of carrying out the functions in which we are engaged.

We believe the material well-being of the American people, as well as the strength of our Company, will in the future, as in the past, be largely dependent upon inventiveness; that prudence requires that we provide funds, facilities and talent for the vigorous pursuit of research in all aspects of our business.

We believe in being a good neighbor by doing our proportionate share, on the basis of ability, in whatever is good for the communities where we do business and by refraining from doing anything that is harmful or detrimental in those communities.

We believe in practicing economical use of natural resources to obtain the greatest possible benefit with the least possible waste.

We believe that in wartime the Military Forces must have prior claim upon our services and products and that our fullest resources must be dedicated to the common defense at such times.

We believe the attitudes of many groups and of the general public toward our business and the oil industry are important to our future; that their attitudes in the main reflect their knowledge or lack of knowledge of what we do and why. Consequently, it is prudent that we explain our business and account for our stewardship in order that people may hold informed opinions and reach wise decisions with respect to public policy as it affects our Company and Industry.

With these principles as our guides, we shall strive to manage our affairs so as to reflect credit upon our Company, our Industry and our Country.

                                                    SUN OIL COMPANY

Six

●

Education—A Debt to Future Generations

"I have over the past years made a careful study of what is being taught in our schools and colleges, and I have been shocked to learn that even in some of our leading universities American ideals are being sabotaged and false ideologies taught. Unless this trend is stopped, we will soon have a generation who will be without the knowledge of the meaning of liberty or individual freedom—the sources from which our great country sprang."*

TO MAKE THE MOST of life, and to make the best of it, this was Howard Pew's concept of living. But this did not mean that he should carry on as chief executive of the company until his last days. There was a natural order of things to which he had to submit. He was convinced that the president of an industrial organization should step down, at age 65, so that a capable leader of the next generation may carry on. To neglect this natural order of succession, just because the old generation has grown accustomed to positions of leadership and power, may jeopardize the future of the company. Therefore, at 65, J. Howard Pew stepped down with great trepidation, but obedient to natural law as he saw it, and made room for the 37-year-old company comptroller, Robert G. Dunlop.

To J. Howard Pew, life derived its value from its use for noble ends. Regardless of his age, for him to live was to act,

*J. Howard Pew, Grove City College Alumni, June 10, 1950.

147

to make use of his senses and faculties, his great experience and wisdom. And so at 65 he embarked upon a new vocation that was to engage his great strength for the rest of his life. He turned from the world of industrial leadership, in which he had performed so magnificently, to the realm of ideas and education, in which he was to give so much to future generations of Americans.

J. Howard Pew was convinced that education is the only cure for the moral and social diseases the modern world has engendered. In fact, the security and destiny of America rest on sound education which, to him, meant instilling profound religious feeling, inspiring true and worthy motives, and inculcating morality under all circumstances. He was guided by the ideals of nineteenth-century education that promoted religion and moral values. In the tradition of the early schools, like Harvard and Dartmouth or many small midwestern colleges with strong denominational influence, Mr. Pew sought to promote education through all media of communication, in schools and seminaries. Daniel Webster had eloquently stated the basic objective: "If we work upon marble, it will perish; if we work upon brass, time will efface it; if we rear temples, they will crumble to dust; but if we work upon men's immortal minds, if we imbue them with high principles, with just fear of God and love of their fellow man, we engrave on these tablets something which no time can efface and which will brighten and brighten to all eternity." (Quoted in a speech to the Grove City College faculty, June 4, 1966, by J. Howard Pew.)

In spite of his great dedication to education with a specific objective, J. Howard Pew strongly resisted another tradition in American private education: the concept of elitist, liberal education. While other private institutions of learning, even those that were originally founded as denominational schools, were designed to teach and influence a select group of affluent Americans, he guided his alma mater, Grove City College,

and directed many other educational endeavors toward edu-
cating every segment of the American people. He rejected the
example set by such eminent schools as Columbia, William
and Mary, Northwestern, Vanderbilt and Stanford, which
educated their students in luxurious fashion and insulated
them from the laboring classes. His great ability and large
wealth were directed at bringing education to the common
man.

J. Howard Pew was an eminent representative of big business which is basic to the economic life of this country. Providing those economic goods and services that constitute the
physical basis of modern living, it also offers the material
foundation for furthering the higher values of man, values
known as "spiritual." It took J. Howard Pew many years of
observation and reflection to arrive at his perception of this
relationship. In an April 24, 1952 speech to the Christian
Freedom Foundation, which he helped to create, he described
his growth in understanding.

"For the first 30 years of my business life, I devoted most of
my time and energy to help make the Company which gave
me employment and success. I wasn't interested in making
money as such, nor in any other business. In 1932 I wak-
ened to the realization that the very foundation of our economy was in jeopardy. Since then I have devoted a perfectly
fabulous amount of my time to a study of economics and kindred subjects. But it is only within the last few years that I
have gradually become conscious of the fact that economics, which is the study of the free market, cannot stand
alone. It must be erected on a Christian foundation. Let me
explain.

"A free market can exist only in a community where the
people generally accept honesty, truthfulness and fairness as
a rule of conduct. But where can you find the attributes of
honesty, truthfulness and fairness except only in a Christian
community?

"My second point has to do with the dignity of man, a biblical concept; and from the dignity of man eventuates freedom, of which the free market is a part. So we see that the two legs which undergird the free market are both Christian.

"Yes, Christianity and freedom are inexorably tied together. If Christianity falls, then freedom is lost—if freedom falls, then Christianity is driven underground. This, briefly put, it seems to me is the philosophy of the Christian Freedom Foundation.

"Morality among the great majority of the politicians has fallen to a very low ebb. It is rare for one of them to advocate a principle which is unpopular, and they resort to all kinds of sophistry to induce voters to support measures designed to deprive them of their freedom.

"On the other hand, the men of the cloth still possess a high sense of honor and integrity. While I may differ from them frequently, I concede that they have been conscientious and honest in arriving at their beliefs. I do not misinterpret their motives.

"I admire the work of the Foundation because it is affirmative and constructive. It is not against any church, denomination or church organization. It seeks to be helpful and cooperative. It attempts to solve its problems by going back to first principles; by developing a creed and then resolving all issues in accordance with that creed. Isn't that the way God would have us do? Isn't that exactly what God intended when He wrote the Ten Commandments on the tablets which Moses carried from the top of Mount Sinai?

"I have had a great many contacts with ministers and clerical groups during these past few years; and I found that the key to the answer to almost every issue is in the Ten Commandments. They certainly constitute the finest and most dependable treatise on economics ever written."

Mr. Pew never implied that the Christian faith has a monopoly on the moral law of God. The official statement of the Christian Freedom Foundation best described his position:

"The moral law of God shines out through all great religions, but is supremely expressed, we believe, by the Christian religion. Its classical statement, is, of course, the Ten Commandments, the Sermon on the Mount and the Golden Rule. Jesus Christ lifted up the law, spiritualized it and wrote it into the hearts of men."

Education, to J. Howard Pew, must always begin with the conscious, methodical dissemination and application of the moral laws to the end that every man may live in accordance with God's order. Education, above all, was spiritual education of all of God's children regardless of race, sex or social origin. He greatly admired the world-wide educational efforts of Billy Graham and supported him in every possible way.

Before the Philadelphia Presbytery, on June 20, 1961, J. Howard Pew gave his unreserved endorsement to Billy Graham. Citing his good old friend Dr. Nelson Bell, who was convinced that Billy Graham was chosen and inspired by God, Pew gave his testimony:

"Dr. Bell is convinced that the success of Billy Graham's preaching is due to four things:

"*Authority*. He does not say what he thinks, nor does he give the opinion of others. He preaches on the authority of the Scriptures, and what 'The Bible says' comes with great conviction.

"The second is *Simplicity*. Most workmen in factories and the average man on the street have a vocabulary of 750 or 800 root words; and many, many of these people have never heard a preacher before whom they understood.

"The third is *Urgency*. Billy preaches with an urgency born of the conviction that men desperately need Jesus Christ as Saviour and Lord.

"Finally, he preaches to a *Decision*. As a good spokesman for Jesus Christ, he presses the claims of Christ as something to be decided on now and not at some distant date.

"To me, Billy's preaching demonstrates three things:

"First, the *Power of Prayer*. Many thousands of people throughout the world are praying for his ministry.

"Second, the *Power of the Holy Spirit*. He knows that only the Holy Spirit can bring about man's conversion.

"Third, the *Power of the Bible* as the sword of the Spirit. To Billy Graham the Bible is the infallible Word of God. He uses it to settle all human affairs, and does it in a most effective manner."

The whole object of J. Howard Pew's efforts in education was to impart moral values and develop the mind so that it may pass moral judgments on human events and actions. To reach the common man and build a broad and popular base he mainly worked through three Christian journals that were very close to his heart: *Christian Economics*, (renamed *Applied Christianity* in 1972), *Christianity Today*, and *The Presbyterian Layman*.

Christian Economics was the first venture into Christian education and proved to be so fruitful and successful that it encouraged the birth of the other two. Howard E. Kershner was its founder in 1950, and Mr. Pew its most loyal supporter. By "Christian economics" they mean that "entrepreneurs operating in the free market will confine their activities to the making and the distribution of such goods and the rendering of such services as will not harm, but on the other hand will benefit their fellows. The free market would sanction prostitution, gambling, pornography and the liquor traffic, but Christian men would not engage in such activities as they consider harmful to their fellows. Christian economics, therefore, requires the free market but goes far beyond to limit the activities of business and professional men to things which are moral and helpful to others."

Christian Economics was organized to set forth and teach the true relationships among freedom, self-government, and economic well-being. In Kershner's words, with which Pew heartily agreed,

"To the extent that the first commandment is observed, men are free. When it is nullified, they are enslaved. Statism is the negation of this Commandment. It makes the state and not God the supreme authority over man.

"In the authoritarian state, which inevitably follows the introduction of 'welfare state' measures requiring more and more socialization until the whole body politic has been collectivized, the state assumes the right to direct the individual and enforces this decision to the most extreme limit. Man is not free to keep the first commandment—to obey God—for he must obey the state. Collectivism, therefore, whether mild or uncompromising, violates the first and great commandment and destroys the liberty of man.

"The materialistic Marxist philosophy of collectivism which denies God would destroy the individual personality or the spiritual nature of man and make him an automaton.

"The first and great commandment marked the emergence of the idea that no man was to be exploited by his fellows. It was a declaration upon which the independence and freedom of the individual were established. It limited the right of the group to control him. It marked the beginning of a long struggle to make good this freedom.

"In sum, morality comes from God. Only men who accept the high moral standards which they attribute to God as rules for their conduct will be fair, honest, just and generous to their fellows. If they are not governed by these high principles, most men will have to live as slaves to the few that are strong. Only moral men can be free. Only eternal commitment to eternal right will prevent the strong from taking what they want at the expense of the weak.

"Freedom, therefore, is based on the spiritual qualities which the Saints and Prophets of all ages have tried to teach us, and which are succinctly summed up in the Ten Commandments."

Since *Christian Economics* proved to be so effective,

reaching hundreds of thousands of concerned readers, J. Howard Pew, together with Billy Graham and Dr. Nelson Bell, set about launching yet another journal of Christian education: *Christianity Today*. Mr. Pew provided most of the financial support and gave it its corporate structure. He faithfully attended every board meeting and helped to shape its editorial policy. Addressing itself mainly to the Protestant clergy the journal endeavored to state the case for theological conservatism. It was to defend and uphold the Protestant principle of Biblical authority, that is, that the Bible, and the Bible alone, is the religion of Protestants. Tradition, creed, and dogma are derived from the Bible, and therefore are not on par with it. Standing in conscious opposition to liberal humanism, *Christianity Today* hopefully was to become not only the vocal organ of theological conservatism, but also the most influential religious journal in America today.

At times, Mr. Pew was disappointed about editorial management that made *Christianity Today* a "forum" instead of an "organ." In fact, in a June 25, 1964 speech to the Board he offered his resignation: "I am the steward of resources which God has entrusted to my care, and as I alone am responsible for making an accounting of the stewardship, I may be compelled to resign from the Board of *Christianity Today.*" The burning issue that, in his judgment, demanded editorial attention was the controversial political, social, and economic statements made by the General Assembly of the Presbyterian Church meeting in Oklahoma City. "The editorial staff of *Christianity Today*," Pew charged, "should not only realize the timeliness of answering this great evil committed by our Church, without any prodding from me or anybody else, but should have been able to answer it much more effectively than I could. But after repeated proddings, they came up with a number of innocuous editorials, all of which were based on the competence and knowledge of the church, the presumption being that if the Church did possess competence and knowledge, it was fully justified in making such economic, social and political statements as they may see fit. Now the facts are, that knowledge and competence are not the issue, but it is clearly one of jurisdiction. This the editorial staff should have known; and their lack of knowledge on this issue alone is sufficient evidence to justify an allegation of incompetence. But this was not all. Even if the issue had been one of competence and knowledge, the way they presented it carried with it no conviction."

A few years later, in 1967, J. Howard Pew launched yet another journal of Christian education aimed at his three million fellow-Presbyterians: *The Presbyterian Layman*. Under the able editorial leadership of James J. Cochran this publication set out to speak constructively to the life and work of the Church from a viewpoint that reflected also the educational objectives of Mr. Pew:

1. To emphasize the teaching of the Bible as the authoritative Word of God;
2. To present Jesus Christ through preaching, teaching, and witnessing with evangelical zeal;
3. For individuals to become involved in the social economic and political affairs of the world;
4. For official Church bodies to "refrain from issuing pronouncements or taking actions unless the authority to speak and act is clearly biblical, the competence of the church body has been established, and all viewpoints have been thoroughly considered."

Meaningful religious education, to J. Howard Pew, meant the dissemination of the moral laws on all levels of education, from the kindergarten to the seminary. This is why he was especially generous in his support of colleges firmly biblical in orientation, such as the Philadelphia College of Bible.

When, in 1969, the Conwell School of Theology in Philadelphia and the Gordon Divinity School of Boston thought to bolster their sagging financial situation by merging, Mr. Pew gave the new institution his hearty support. The two seminaries began to operate as a single institution in the fall of 1969 as Gordon-Conwell Theological Seminary with Mr. Pew's good friend, Dr. Harold Ockenga, as President. Believing that under his leadership this multidenominational institution would become one of the leading seminaries in the country, Mr. Pew purchased the beautiful Carmelite property from the Roman Catholic Church in South Hamilton, Massachusetts, to be used as its new campus. It is significant that none of the buildings on campus bear his name.

As a correlative to this transaction, the vacated site formerly occupied by the Conwell School of Theology in Philadelphia was now available. Mr. Pew purchased it and gave it to a black group that wished to train black ministers. Unfortunately, the group that took charge were more political than theological in orientation, which probably caused it to fail soon after Mr. Pew's death.

Long before the education of racial minorities became the acid test of the American conscience, long before the 1954 Brown decision of the Supreme Court outlawed the separate-but-equal principle that had permitted dual white and black school systems, J. Howard Pew supported Negro education. His high moral objectives left no room for racial pride or prejudice. His own alma mater, Grove City College, which he served as Chairman of the Board from 1931 until his death, had been integrated since its beginning in 1876. As soon as the Pew Memorial Trust was organized in 1948 and made grants to educational institutions, Negro education received a considerable share of its financial resources. Large grants were made not only to the United Negro College Fund, but also to a number of black colleges, such as Hampton Institute in Hampton, Virginia, Bishop College in Dallas, Texas, and St. Augustine's College in Raleigh, N.C.

The great zeal that made J. Howard Pew so successful in his business career also afforded him great success in his educational efforts. Giving himself to his work, body and soul, his life was a shining example that inspired courage and gave guidance to the productive labors of many kindred souls. And yet, he never looked down on others, but on himself in humility which gave him understanding of his fellowmen. It afforded him the wisdom of age and the youthful ability to learn anew as long as he lived. Whereas many of his contemporaries retired from active life for leisure and contemplation, he sought new knowledge and found new challenges that demanded all his strength and ability.

He found hope and inspiration from the work of Leonard Read and the Foundation for Economic Education whose Board he joined in 1950. The Foundation's unique educational method, which was so attractive to Pew, is its inner-direction, its emphasis on self-improvement. Individuals who voluntarily associate with it are seeking a better understanding of the freedom philosophy, that is, knowledge of the market economy, the private property order, limited government, and their moral and spiritual antecedents. The Foundation and its many thousands of disciples the world over are seeking greater knowledge in the moral, social and economic laws that encompass human lives, and are exploring ways of explaining them with ever-improving clarity. Its monthly study journal, *The Freeman,* offers an opportunity to skilled expositors to share their understanding of freedom with many thousands of fellow students.

The moral and spiritual antecedents of individual freedom that are emphasized by the Foundation constituted the very foundation of J. Howard Pew's philosophy. Leonard Read's works such as *Accent on the Right,* and *Students of Liberty,* and staff member Rev. Edmund A. Opitz' *Religion and Capitalism—Allies not Enemies,* reflected Pew's educational priorities and formed the bond of mutual respect and friendship. Besides his financial support to FEE he gave unstintingly of his great strength, his keen mind and wise counsel.

To open the gates to virtue J. Howard Pew depended on

education. College education was merely supplementary to family education and order, and was to develop the mind so that it was able to pass moral judgments and make right decisions. This, to him, was the very purpose and aspiration of Grove City College, his alma mater and his alma custodia for most of his adult life.

With the exception of brief periods, this College is the life and work of two men: Dr. Isaac Ketler and his son, Dr. Weir C. Ketler. Isaac Ketler created the institution in 1876, and nurtured it through its growing pains. Joseph Newton Pew joined him as President of the Board in 1895 when the College was reorganized along eleemosynary lines. Weir C. Ketler built a modern institution with a beautiful plant on the solid foundation laid by his father.

Upon Weir C. Ketler's retirement in 1956, the Board, under J. Howard Pew's chairmanship, elected Rev. J. Stanley Harker, a GCC alumnus of 1925, President of the College. He served with dedication and ability until his retirement in 1971, when Rev. Charles S. MacKenzie assumed the Presidency. J. Howard Pew, although stricken by his terminal illness, helped to select this young president who is now guiding the College along the proven path.

The great ideals and principles of Grove City College, which J. Howard Pew served first as member and then as Chairman of the Board for more than fifty-nine years, reflect the greatness of its founders and the dreams and aspirations of its most illustrious trustee.

1. A belief in God, the Father Almighty, who has endowed all men as Persons, not as creatures, with certain inalienable rights, among these being Life, Liberty and the pursuit of Happiness.
2. A belief that the family and home constitute the foundation of our society and that the preservation and promotion of their integrity are paramount to the welfare of mankind.

3. A belief that social justice and the rights of men are best served by a representative republican form of government, deriving its just powers from consent of the governed, as established by our Constitution.

4. A belief that all men and women should be equal before the law and in the economic, educational, political and military life of the country.

5. A belief in freedom of religion, freedom of speech, freedom of press and radio, the right of the people peaceably to assemble and to petition the government for a redress of their grievances.

6. A belief that no citizen shall be deprived of life, liberty or property without due process of law and just compensation for property taken from him.

7. A belief that each individual should have freedom and opportunity to exercise his talents and industry in any way which does not injure the general welfare, and should be rewarded according to the value of his service.

8. A belief that progress depends on production and plenty, not on a planned economy of scarcity; that there is no foreseeable limit to our expanding frontiers in technological improvements and advances; and that we must look in this direction to assure the opportunities which the youth of America deserve.

9. A belief that these ends can be attained only through private competitive enterprise and the free flow of trade and commerce among the States.

10. A belief that the best results in education can be attained through a clear understanding of these principles.

Throughout his long association with GCC Mr. Pew frequently spoke about these principles. In countless speeches to students, instructors, and alumni he urged his listeners to hold fast to the College ideals. In a speech to the Pittsburgh alumni on Oct. 21, 1949, he emphasized his belief "that the peace, prosperity and security of this Nation depend more on our colleges and universities than on any other agency. I doubt that any alien forces can upset our national security without first undermining our spiritual, moral and intellectual foundations. Our colleges must be kept strong, for they

are our outposts. At Grove City College we stress the value
of religious, political and economic liberty. Our priceless
liberty is recognized as the very cornerstone of American
civilization. It is our most precious heritage. The education
of our youth to a full appreciation of our heritage is the only
safeguard against the destruction of our American institutions. To teach this appreciation of our liberty and the recognition of the forces that threaten it, will always be the fore-
most mission of this College."

He took great pride in the managerial efficiency with which
the College was operating. At the annual Board-faculty
luncheons that precede the baccalaureate services he would
proudly announce that once again the College was "still sol-
vent" and operating in the black. He would report that the
expenses of tuition, board and room were the lowest of any
comparable college in the East, and that nevertheless College
revenue defrayed operating and maintenance expenses.

At times he would also relate that the College plant repre-
sented an educational investment of many thousands of dollars per student, which was "a considerably greater investment than that of any other private college in the State." The
costs of this capital investment formed no part of his calcu-
lation of operating expenses—the needed capital was to be
raised and defrayed by the trustees and friends of the College.
In an address to the GCC alumni, on June 3, 1961, which this
writer was privileged to hear, J. Howard Pew probably revealed his own feeling of obligation and vision of the future
of his beloved college.

"When I look over this campus and see these magnificent
buildings which have been constructed to last indefinitely, I
am reminded of an incident which occurred in early English
history. In the year 1379, New College of Oxford University
was founded by the Earl of Wickham, a conscientious and
dedicated churchman. In those days, the founder of a college
usually supplied, not only the materials for its construction,

but the capital for its support. Five hundred years after the founding of the college, the oak beams in the great hall needed to be replaced. In those days, as now, the college was faced with the problem of securing the finances for such a project. Someone suggested that the descendants of the Earl of Wickham might be interested in continuing the tradition of the college by providing the funds for this purpose. And so a committee called upon the members of the Wickham family and, after explaining the purpose of their visit, were amazed at their cordial reception and the answer that was immediately forthcoming: 'The trees are ready for you,' they said. And then they related that when the Earl of Wickham founded the college, he planted a large grove of oak trees, having in mind that when the beams needed to be replaced, the trees would be ready for the purpose. Here was a five-century vision."

The strikingly beautiful campus of Grove City College tells its own glorious story of the vision of it genius founder, Isaac Ketler, its great builder, Weir C. Ketler, and of its generous benefactors, such as the Harbison, the Crawford and the Pew families. But it is far more than perfection of living appointments, of beauty and charm. To J. Howard Pew his alma mater also was an ideal concept of mental and moral improvement, a concept that reveals man's deficiencies and spurs him on to higher and better things. It was an ideal that was derived from the unchanging law of God and the principles of eternal morality and justice, which are the very foundation of a moral and civilized society.

> Truth, Honor, Justice! The great trinity
> We learned to cherish in thy hallowed halls.[12]

---

[12]*J. Howard Pew, as quoted in an address to Founder's Day Assembly, April 11, 1951.*

Seven

●

Wealth as God's Gift and Trust

"Charity as practiced in this country today originated almost 2,000 years ago, at the last supper which Christ had with His disciples, when, after Judas left on his mission of betrayal, Christ said: 'A new commandment I give unto you, That ye love one another; as I have loved you, that ye also love one another.'"°

IN SOME DEGREE we all are beneficiaries of philanthropy when we attend a church, go to a private school or college, visit a museum or listen to a concert, borrow a book from a library, stroll through a public park, or receive treatment in a hospital. We use institutions and services that may be tax-supported today, but were originated in the distant past as philanthropic enterprises. In fact, the record of American philanthropy in the fields of charity, religion, education, social service, war relief, and foreign aid is so impressive that many books have been written about its achievements.

The roots of American philanthropy grew in early colonial times when Puritan leaders, such as John Winthrop, preached about charity as a code of conduct for Christians who had entered into a covenant with God. To William Penn and the Quakers, help and countenance to unfortunate fellowmen was as important to religious living as formal worship. God's stewardship meant that man was indebted to God not only for his very being but also for his earthly possessions, and was accountable to Him for the way he spent his life as well as his fortune.

°J. Howard Pew Remarks at Jefferson Medical College, 1952.

162

During the 18th and 19th centuries, when large fortunes were still a novelty, most American philanthropists gave out of this feeling of religious duty, to discharge their obligations of stewardship faithfully. It was also J. Howard Pew's motive in supporting a great variety of worthy causes. Confident that his prosperity came from God and, therefore, free of any feelings of guilt, he managed his great fortune as the good steward who, at the appointed hour, sought to be ready to give a final account.

To J. Howard Pew, charity was one of the triad of Christian virtues, together with faith and hope. It was originally chartered under Christ's great commandment "That ye love one another," and called forth by the giving love of God for man as set forth by the life and death of His Son. In a 1952 address to the students and instructors of Jefferson Medical College in Philadelphia Mr. Pew explained this commandment:

"Words have a way of changing their meaning, with the passage of time. Frequently words are replaced, in whole or in part, by new words. During the life of Christ there was only one word to denote charity and love; charity being a work of love, was not distinguished from love itself.

"The King James' version of the Holy Bible was completed in 1610. The meaning of so many of our old English words have so changed during these 350 years, that it became necessary to have a new revised version of the Holy Bible. This has just been completed and is now on the press.

"In the King James' version that famous passage in Saint Paul's letter to the Corinthians reads: 'And now abideth faith, hope, charity, these three; but the greatest of these is charity.' The new revised version: 'So faith, hope, love abide, these three; and the greatest of these is love.

"And so this task to which you are devoting so much of your time and energy is a work of love, originally chartered under Christ's great commandment, 'That ye love one another.'"

J. Howard Pew was convinced that every good act is love and charity. The good we do in this world to our fellowmen is our work of love as chartered under the great commandment. The physician's skill and knowledge that save human lives or soothe the suffering of the sick are charity in action. Talking to the medical students he dwelled on the giant strides made by the medical profession during the last few generations, that "the span of human life has increased over 20 years; most of the diseases that plagued our parents and our grandparents have now been almost eliminated; and literally millions of lives are being saved every year by abdominal operations.

"A typical story illustrating how this was accomplished, is that of Ephraim McDowell. One hundred forty years ago Ephraim McDowell was a practicing physician in Danville, Kentucky, then a small hamlet on the edge of the wilderness. A few days before Christmas he was summoned 60 miles to see a patient, a Mrs. Crawford. The local doctor had told her that she was pregnant; but after 10 or 11 months had passed, her condition became so alarming that Dr. McDowell was called into consultation. He diagnosed her case as ovarian tumor. No surgeon had ever dared operate in such a case, because it was popularly believed that the contact of the outside atmosphere with the interior of the abdominal cavity meant certain death.

"Dr. McDowell had long believed such an operation possible; and so he persuaded Mrs. Crawford to let him do it. The operation had to be performed at the doctor's home, where he had all of his surgical equipment. So she accompanied him on horseback the 60 miles back to Danville, suffering excruciating pain at every step.

"When it became known in the village that this operation was to be performed, feeling ran high against Dr. McDowell. The people decided the operation must be stopped, either by law or by a mob, if necessary. But Dr. McDowell was undaunted. Even though he knew the operation might result in the death of his patient—and certain death to him if the operation failed—nevertheless he was prepared to take the risk.

"The operation was performed on Christmas morning. When the services in the local church were over, the people from the village gathered in front of the doctor's home and, with a rope around a tree, were prepared to hang him just as soon as the patient died. And then, becoming impatient, they tried to break into the house but were stopped by the sheriff.

"All this was before the development of anesthesia, but legend has it that Mrs. Crawford sang hymns to drown out the pain while the doctor worked. Anyhow, despite the screams of the patient in the inside and the howls of the mob on the outside, Dr. McDowell performed the first abdominal operation in the history of medicine. Not only did the patient survive, but she lived to be over 80 years of age. Dr. McDowell's fame became widespread. Later he was called to Tennessee to perform a similar operation on the wife of a friend of Andrew Jackson; and Old Hickory himself handed him the instruments during the operation."

When, in 1950, J. Howard Pew's wife fell sick with a mysterious blood disease, he practically retired from business to care for her. He got the best medical advice from blood experts the world over who eventually discovered the cause of the disease and found a cure. Like a young medical student or research assistant, J. Howard read a great deal on blood and circulation, kept notes on her and gathered scientific information on the symptoms of the disease. Thus, armed with many volumes of information and expert opinions from all over the world, J. Howard was desirous that everyone should benefit from the research. He engaged Dr. Irvin Moon of the Moody Science Films in Chicago to produce the film *The Red River of Life*. It is an outstanding film on the functions of blood that continues to be in demand by interested groups all over the country. And J. Howard would talk for hours to anyone of his visitors on the operation of the blood stream, like a professor of medicine at Jefferson Medical College.

Mr. Pew, who was charitable and indulgent to everyone but himself, distinguished between two kinds of charity, remedial and productive. He approached the former with great care and thought, lest his gifts be injurious to the recipients. The latter, to him, was always beneficial and praiseworthy. It encompassed every individual effort toward the spiritual, intellectual and economic betterment of our fellowmen. The greatest economic charity, to him, was every productive effort that enables other individuals to become independent of alms. Inversely, bad charity, to him, was that alm which takes from independence its pride and from mendicity its shame.

J. Howard Pew rejected the humanistic attitude that attaches primary importance to man, to his affairs, aspirations and well-being. Although he frequently spoke about the greatness of man's potentials, especially when addressing students and youth groups, he believed that men and women everywhere needed to be saved and taught the message of salvation. His commandment was the Bible, as God's inspired, inerrant and infallible word. To him man was not the measure of all things; his focus was on God and His church.

Philanthropy, to J. Howard Pew, obviously was no handmaid of political, social or economic reform, not even an antidote for radical proposals for distributing private wealth. Unequal distribution of income and wealth resulted from the inequalities of individual ability and productivity. Any attempt to erase that inequality would violate God's order and bring ruin to all. There was no "surplus wealth," merely productive wealth that produces economic goods and renders services to millions of fellowmen, and consumptive wealth that sustains life, health, and well-being. The Pews always lived humbly, spending little on themselves. More than ninety per cent of their income was given to philanthropic causes.

Not for himself, but for his stewardship he managed his great fortune. Upon retirement from company management he devoted much of his time to administering his income wisely and beneficially. As little charitable giving is direct from the donor to the object of need, charity organizations and agencies act as intermediaries. They present their requests in person or writing, frequently with the aid of a professional fund-raising firm. On many days Mr. Pew would receive dozens of written requests for charitable assistance and listen to the pleas of twenty to thirty fund-raisers who beat a path to his office door in the Sun Oil building. He was quite willing to give, but as a good steward he felt an obligation to inquire into the causes to which he was asked to contribute. These investigations took more of his time and energy than the affairs of Sun Oil Company.

To administer their charitable efforts more efficiently, the four Pew brothers and sisters, in 1948, established the Pew Memorial Foundation to which they contributed 800,000 shares of Sun Oil common stock. Over the years, the original donations grew with stock dividends, stock splits and more donations to some 6.5 million shares, valued at more than four hundred million dollars, or nearly one-half the estimated family fortune of $900 million, at the time of J. Howard's death.

The Foundation is a broad-purpose charitable trust that, over the years, has made grants to practically all facets of social life. It has supported the United Fund, the Boy Scouts, Girl Scouts, YMCA and YWCA, the Red Cross, independent colleges, hospitals and medical research, religious causes and crusades, Bible colleges and seminaries, and so on. In addition, two other trusts, called the J. Howard Pew Freedom Trust, with assets of some $15 million, and the J. N. Pew, Jr. Charitable Trust, with assets of some $50 million, are used to support philanthropic causes. All three are administered by the Glenmede Trust Company, as trustee, which occupies an office in the Sun Oil Company headquarters building in Philadelphia. Its president, Allyn R. Bell, Jr., afforded J. Howard valuable assistance in his benefactions by interviewing supplicants, making inquiries, and suggesting action.

The greatest danger to Christian charity, according to Mr. Pew, loomed in the rise of compulsory benevolence by an omnipotent provider state. Where government permits no free institutions, charitable services previously supported by private benevolence are maintained by taxation and controlled by government. But public bodies are not able to undertake the philanthropic tasks which a great number of private charities can accomplish. Above all, while voluntary activity strengthens social goodwill and cooperation, the coercive redistribution by the state not only breeds corruption and waste, but also generates social division and conflict. There can be no progress where planning boards and government controls tend to destroy individual ingenuity, incentive, resourcefulness, and invention.

In his speech mentioned above, Mr. Pew reflected on this great danger.

"In Russia today all private societies have been eliminated. Every organization of any kind whatsoever is now state controlled. Before the revolution much of the charity was carried on by the local parishes. Most of the charity was conducted by the Greek Orthodox Church. When the churches were closed, these charities were closed. Since then a few of the churches have been allowed to open but they are forbidden to engage in any activity except only that of conducting an occasional church service. The Soviet Red Cross, no longer a member of the International Red Cross, has been put under government control and limited to doing a restricted service for the Russian Army. The Salvation Army, the Boy Scouts, and the Tolstoy groups have been liquidated.

"In Poland all private hospitals have been eliminated; all schools have been put under the control of the Party; and the medical associations have been disbanded. In Czechoslovakia, Jugoslavia, Bulgaria, Lithuania, Esthonia and Hungary all private charities of every kind have ceased to exist. It is fair to say that all charities of every kind behind the Iron Curtain have been eliminated except only the few which remain in East Germany.

"In England, where economic planning and government controls have not been quite so severe as they have been behind the Iron Curtain, most charities were eliminated when the government socialized the welfare agencies.

"What of the future? Charity, a work of love, can exist only where it is free. It is freedom that has effected the miracle of America—intellectual freedom, religious freedom, political freedom, industrial freedom; freedom to dream, to think, to experiment, to invent, to match wits in friendly competition; freedom to be an individual. That is our great American heritage. But freedom is indivisible. Thus if we should lose any one of our freedoms, all the rest would certainly fall.

"The great English statesman, Disraeli, once said: 'The health of a people is really the foundation upon which all their happiness and all their powers as a State depend.' I need not remind you that the 'State of the Union' was conceived here in Philadelphia, and the powers we enjoy as the free people of a free nation are derived from the Constitution which was written here. We of Philadelphia should be constantly on guard in preserving the foundations of that State, and should pioneer in the preservation of the health of its people. It is a sacred trust, inherited from our Founding Fathers. With the threat of socialized medicine a constant menace, let us redouble our efforts to safeguard that sacred trust, and pray that Jefferson Hospital may prove a bulwark against the creeping paralysis of government control over medicine.

"Christ's own commandment, to love one another, was the inspiration for the founding of Jefferson Hospital. Jefferson Hospital can exist only so long as our form of government permits free institutions. At this critical time in our country's history, when the whole structure of freedom is in jeopardy, it is vitally important that free institutions, such as Jefferson, should be maintained and enlarged from time to time to meet the requirements of the community which they serve.

Let me close by repeating the warning of William Penn, the founder of this great Commonwealth, when he said: 'Men will either be governed by God or ruled by tyrants.'"

J. Howard Pew's will, which was dated November 11, 1963, was, in the true sense, a testament: a final declaration of faith and philosophy and his prayer for God's blessing upon the American people. He expressed the wish that his estate go essentially toward the support of tax-exempt religious, charitable, scientific, literary or educational institutions best calculated, in the judgment of the Trustee, to "inculcate in the minds and hearts of the American people the true concepts of individual liberty and freedom."

More specifically, Mr. Pew said he hoped the Trustee would "accord consideration" to institutions and organizations, of the character he specified, which utilize educational means—

"To acquaint the American people with the evils of bureaucracy and the vital need to maintain and preserve a limited form of government in the United States as intended by our forebears and expressed by them in the Constitution and the Bill of Rights—to point out the dangerous consequences that result from an exchange of our American priceless heritage of freedom and self-determination, for the false promises of Socialism and a planned economy—to expose the insidious influences which have infiltrated many of our channels of publicity—and to inform our people of the struggle, persecution, hardship, sacrifice and death by which freedom of the individual was won.

"To acquaint the American people with the values of a free market—the dangers of inflation—the need for a stable monetary standard—the paralyzing effects of government controls on the lives and activities of people—and the necessity of maintaining the rights as provided in the Bill of Rights.

"To promote recognition of the interdependence of Christianity and freedom and to support and expound the philosophy that we must first have faith in God before we can enjoy the blessings of liberty—for God is the author of liberty—and to bring about the realization that our failure to fight for the preservation of our liberty is a crime, the punishment for which is servitude."

J. Howard Pew was a builder—of a great company, many institutions of learning, numerous charities, and above all his beloved church. He often recited a particular poem that sheds some light on his soul and genius:

THE BRIDGE BUILDER
by Will Allen Dromgoole

An old man traveling a lone highway,
Came at evening, cold and gray,
To a chasm deep and wide,
Through which there flowed a sullen tide.
The old man crossed in the twilight dim,
For the sullen stream held no fear for him.
He turned when he reached the other side
And built a bridge to span the tide.

"Old man!" cried a fellow pilgrim near,
"Why waste your strength with your building here;
Your journey will end with the ending day,
And you never again will pass this way;
You have crossed the chasm deep and wide,
Why build a bridge at eventide?"

The builder raised his old gray head,
"Good friend, on the path I have come," he said,
"There followeth after me today
A youth whose feet will pass this way.
This stream which has meant naught to me,
To that fair-haired boy may a pitfall be;
He, too, must cross in the twilight dim.
Good friend, I am building this bridge for him."

INDEX

173